W9-DIU-167

F V

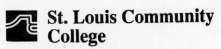
St. Louis Community College

Forest Park
Florissant Valley
Meramec

Instructional Resources
St. Louis, Missouri

Galloping Bungalows

Galloping Bungalows

THE RISE AND
DEMISE OF THE
AMERICAN
HOUSE
TRAILER

DAVID A. THORNBURG

ARCHON BOOKS 1991

The paper used in this publication meets the minimum
requirements of American National Standard for Information
Sciences—Permanence of Paper for Printed Materials, ANSI
Z39.48–1984 ∞

Library of Congress Cataloging-in-Publication Data

Thornburg, David A., 1942–
Galloping bungalows : the rise and demise of
the American house trailer / David A. Thornburg
p.   cm.
Includes bibliographical references and index.
1. Mobile homes—United States—History.
2. Mobile home living—United States—History.
I. Title.
TL297.T56   1990   643′2.—dc20   90-41214
ISBN 0-208-02277-5

Photos, except where otherwise credited in individual
captions, courtesy Library of Congress.

Book design by Nancy Ovedovitz

Contents

This was a peaceful place, this camp—a Garden of Eden on wheels, capable of picking its own latitudes and following the gentle weather round the year, a haven in which every occupant had brought his life into focus by compressing it into the minimum space, a miracle of internal arrangement plus mobility.

—E. B. White, *Harper's Monthly,* May 1941

In the United States there is more space where nobody is than where anybody is.

This is what makes America what it is.

—Gertrude Stein, *The Geographical History of America*

. . . with a strange whale behind his fish-shaped car. . . .

—Lawrence Saunders, *The Saturday Evening Post,* May 23, 1936

for Dave and Emily

Introduction

We Americans are obsessed with freedom: the mere mention of the word makes us want to start singing songs and waving flags or gun barrels around. But the plain fact is, any time one of our neighbors actually begins to get a little freedom—begins to rise up out of the flock and flap a tentative wing—it first makes us nervous, and then jealous, and finally angry. Immediately we begin casting about for some law or lasso to bring him back to earth.

When the house trailer first came to the public's attention in the summer of 1935, America was adrift, desperately in need of a new dream. The twenties' dream of wealth unlimited had died with the Wall Street crash of '29, and nothing had come along to replace it. The gold had all been mined, the railroads built, the West settled. Only Alaska remained open and free—but Alaska, in the thirties, was as cold and distant as the moon. We were a nation frozen in time. From Maine to California nothing seemed to be moving except the rolling dark clouds of Depression, and all America sat on its front porch, listening to Roosevelt, rocking listlessly and eyeing the weather, holding its breath and waiting for something to happen.

And then a car rolled past—a neighbor's car, headed for Florida. And fastened to its bumper was a brand-new camping trailer—except that it was bigger and gaudier than a camping trailer had any right to be. Inside was a living room and a kitchen and a folding bed, a stove and a sink and a toilet and a new-fangled "showerbath." Why, the thing was a miniature house on wheels! Sleek and fancy as a yacht—a land yacht! You could actually live in one of these contraptions, and travel around and see the country—more cheaply, some said, than you could stay home. Three hundred thousand people were already doing so.

Now here was something moving, at least; something going somewhere. Just think of it: a brand-new life style, built around a rolling home! Why, it could take you to the woods on weekends. It could

1

take you down to Miami for the winter. It could take you all the way to California, if you liked. Comfortably and cheaply. So comfortably, in fact, that a lot of people who spent a week or two in a trailer didn't want to move back into their old-fashioned house or apartment—didn't want to give up this new life of carefree simplicity, of fresh air and freedom. They found that they liked being able to choose new neighbors at will; liked not having a garage to paint, a yard to mow, a basement to clean. They liked the idea of south for the winter, north for the summer—liked it so well that they sold their house and furniture, hit the road, and became full-time "trailerites."

And so, right out of the heart of the Great Depression a new dream was born: the trailer dream, the dream of escape. Escape from snow and ice, from high taxes and rent, from an economic system that nobody trusted anymore. Escape! For the weekend, for the winter, for the rest of your life. All it took was a little courage and a six-hundred-dollar house trailer.

Not your boxy, cumbersome, immobile mobile home of today, mind you—that's another whole way of life. The house trailer was the mobile home's lithe and winsome little ancestor, a sleek plywood cabin on wheels, a one-room doll house big enough to sleep four, yet small enough to follow a forty-horsepower Ford up the back side of Wartburg Mountain and right down into Knoxville. A galloping bungalow.

Didn't Clark Gable and Carole Lombard already own one? And W. C. Fields? And Andy Devine, and Gypsy Rose Lee? Dorothy Parker and Sinclair Lewis had honeymooned in theirs. And that dashing movie star and pilot, Wallace Beery—wasn't he a trailerite? Old Henry Ford himself, and Dr. Charles Mayo of the Mayo Clinic, too. Why, they say William K. Vanderbilt's trailer had three bathrooms and servants' quarters! *Everyone* was buying them. It was the smart thing for the smart set to do, in the year 1936.

So how is it that the house trailer, which began life so hopefully, began life dancing chic to chic with industrialists and movie stars, came to be the pariah, the unmentionable, the leper of American housing? Where did all that promise, all that romance go? How did the very word "trailer" come to be synonymous with slum?

When I mentioned to a neighbor, an insurance broker from Manhattan, that I was writing about the five million Americans who once

> "Living in a trailer is a lot of fun. There is always a sort of picnic feel, for one thing. A sort of holiday air. It makes you feel you're living on a perpetual vacation, even if you're not. You're much closer to the outdoors than you are in a house."
> —James Jones, author of *From Here to Eternity*

lived in house trailers, he was at no loss for words. "That makes me nauseous!" he exclaimed. "I'm a solid citizen, and that just makes me *nauseous!*" Trailers do that to some people. I found out early in my research that I couldn't just sit down next to strangers, and tell them what I was doing, and ask if any of their family had ever lived on wheels. The reaction was much the same as if I'd said, "Say, I'm writing this book about prison life. Have you or any of your relatives. . . ." And yet almost everyone I meet turns out to have had an uncle or a grandmother or a friend who lived in one of these curious little flying flats—but the memory is buried so deep that it takes an hour of conversation, or a few old photographs, to shake it loose.

People who grow up in ghettos are often proud of their background. As soon as they escape they begin to boast, like Ben Franklin at the Court of Versailles, of their humble beginnings, their "leather-apron days." But I've never heard anyone except myself admit that he or she was born in a house trailer, or mention living on a trailer court, which was a peculiar kind of ghetto for one of the most despised and misunderstood minority groups this country has ever spawned—the American trailerite.

And yet the early trailerites, the people who gave up their houses to live full time in those fragile little gypsy wagons, as my parents did from 1940 to 1955, were a hardy and admirable breed, true pioneer stock—at once wildly rebellious and typically middle American in their values and mores. Like so many pioneers, they were dissatisfied with the present, so they set off in search of the past—and inadvertently paved the road to the future. They had a dream—a sentimental, Arcadian dream of sunshine and neighborliness and simple self-sufficiency. And despite a depression and a world war, a lot of them managed to live it.

They're gone now, those five million indigenous American gypsies, and so is the way of life they created. Sometime during the 1950s, the narrow road they were traveling came abruptly to a fork. One branch led straight to the mobile home villa of today, with its chlorinated swimming pool, its nine-hole golf course, its security guard at the gate. The other branch led to a barren and overpriced campground beside some noisy interstate. The old-time trailerites, casual and cantankerous and fiercely independent souls, weren't comfortable or welcome in either place, and so they simply ceased to be—sold their rigs and faded quietly back into the mainstream and were forgotten. Their little hand-crafted plywood dreamboats—homes so tiny that people today mistake them for travel trailers, mere vacation toys—are moldering away unnoticed in farmers' fields, in junkyards, in woodlots and weedlots all across America. And their story, until now, has never been told.

Hope it doesn't make you nauseous.

1 Mister Sherman and His Covered Wagons

Stanfield Oregon Aug 28. One of the recent sights seen along the Columbia River Highway was an ox-team and covered-wagon outfit on its way from Connecticut to California. The wagon was fixed up with an acetylene lighting and heating apparatus and was equipped with a radio outfit with aerials on top of the wagon.

—Christian Science Monitor,
Thursday, August 28, 1924

Five years ago the trailer was just a convenience for motor-tourists, an overnight shelter usually made in the back lot at home, into a sort of mobile bedroom limping along behind the family's battered runabout.

—Literary Digest
November 14, 1936

What good is a history too long for *Newsweek*? The history of the house trailer really begins with the covered carts and wagons used by pre-historic nomads who wandered the steppes of Asia. Four-thousand-year-old models of these ox-drawn vehicles have been unearthed in Syria and Assyria, some of them looking surprisingly like nineteenth-century Conestogas. But for our purposes, the trailer story begins in a suburb of Detroit, Michigan, at the height of the Roaring Twenties, an era of short skirts and free love and bootleg gin.

Mr. Arthur George Sherman was a large man with a prematurely gray cowlick, wire-rimmed glasses, and five children at home. He was a solid family man, and he wasn't particularly interested in short skirts or free love or bootleg gin. He wasn't even interested in a second career, though as it turned out he was teetering on the verge of one. Mr. Sherman simply wanted to go fishing.

He was thirty-eight, the president of his father's Detroit pharmaceutical firm: Sherman Laboratories, makers of serums for colds and pneumonia. It was mid-July of the sweltering summer of 1928, just a year after Lindbergh had hopped the Atlantic. The Big Bull Market was raging on Wall Street, and a plump, cigar-smoking Republican named Herbert Hoover already had the November election in his pocket. Millions of Americans had colds and pneumonia, and millions more were sure to get them. Life was good. What better time for a modern medicine man to take the wife and kids away for a few days of camping and fishing in upper Michigan to forget the cares of the world?

So Sherman went out and bought the most exotic camping gadget that a conservative midwestern businessman of 1928 could imagine: a de luxe tent-trailer that unfolded, petal by petal, into a luxurious, waterproof canvas cabin, in ten minutes or less. The illustrated brochure told you exactly how. The waterproof feature was useful, because it rains buckets in upper Michigan. The ten-minute feature was good, too, because it was raining buckets when the Shermans rolled into the campground. Stuffing the illustrated brochure into his pocket, Sherman stepped manfully out of the family Buick to erect his new toy.

For over an hour he sloshed about, unfolding petals, hoisting poles, wrestling with wet waterproof canvas. His wife got out and helped. The kids got out and helped. The wind blew. The rain continued. The illustrated brochure got soaked through.

A few years later the *Christian Science Monitor* repeatedly referred to Arthur Sherman as an engineer. Sherman was not an engineer—he was a bacteriologist. *Fortune* and *Reader's Digest* called him "another Henry Ford." He wasn't that, either. He was just a tall, quiet family man with a stubborn jawline—a man who couldn't assemble a damned expensive tent-trailer contraption in the rain, with his wife and five kids watching.

The experience angered Sherman, so he went home and designed himself a camp trailer that didn't need assembling—a little masonite bungalow on wheels. It was a simple box, six feet wide by nine feet long, and no taller than the family Buick. It was ugly and cramped, but it had a solid, waterproof roof, and you didn't have to unfold it every time you needed it. He hired a carpenter to build it for him, and

Rolling out: a car and trailer leaving Sarasota (Florida) municipal trailer park, one of the oldest parks in America, in 1940. In the background is the outfield fence of Payne Field, winter home of the Boston Red Sox.

when total strangers offered to buy it, he hired another carpenter, had some more built, and sold them at a profit. Then he bought some more masonite and hired some more carpenters and, by the mid-thirties, people who weren't calling Sherman "an engineer" or "another Henry Ford" were beginning to think of him as the father of the American trailer industry.

And that he was.

Arthur Sherman didn't invent the house trailer, of course, any more than Ford invented the car, or the Wright brothers the airplane. The house trailer is as old as the automobile itself. And the basic idea—a bedroom on wheels—is far older than history. If the house trailer had a family tree, that tree would have to include the horse-drawn wagons of a hundred generations of traders and gypsies and circus performers, houseboats and yachts, sheepherders' wagons, the private railway coaches and lumbering "house-cars" of the wealthy, the tattered wagons and ramshackle trailers of the nineteenth-century wagon tramp and his direct descendent, the auto-tramp of the teens and twenties. And, of course, a whole generation of folding tent-trailers like the one that frustrated Mr. Sherman.

A venerable family tree, stretching back across all of human history—for man has always had a little gypsy blood. But, like most family trees, the trailer's is not exactly topheavy with royalty, for the world's poor have always been more mobile than its rich. The wealthy may be equally at home in their town house or their country estate, but the poor—the mobile poor, at least—tend to be at home wherever they hang their hat.

Still, the automobile trailer didn't begin life as housing for the poor. It began as a camping vehicle, a playtoy for the rich and the near-rich. And it began not in America but in Great Britain. The very first trailers on record appeared in the south of England, about 1906: small, flimsy wooden boxes on cart wheels, bolted—or sometimes merely wired—to the rear bumpers of frail little ten-horsepower Austins and Rovers. Having invented them, the English felt they had a perfect right to name these new creations, and so they did. Without consulting anyone on this side of the Atlantic, they labeled them "motor caravans."

And why not? They were two-wheeled copies of the old one-horse Gypsy caravan, a wooden shack-wagon that housed a cookstove and bunks, two or three adults, and half-a-dozen lively, dark-eyed children. Your really proper Gypsy caravan would have a paint job as gaudy as a neon rainbow, a distinct odor of boiling onions, and a matched pair of whippets tied underneath and trotting patiently along in the dusty shade. Such vehicles were invariably pulled by "the finest piece of 'orseflesh in all of Hengland, Guv'nor"—which just happened to be available for sale or trade. Gypsy caravans have been a common sight along British roadsides since well before Shakespeare's time; wander far enough off the Motorway today and you may yet encounter one.

So the English get the credit—or the blame—for inventing the trailer, even if they didn't know what to call it. But the poky little

"No one knows who built the first trailer, but it was probably a chap who tired of strapping suitcases and miscellaneous baggage to running boards and roof."
—*Popular Mechanics,*
December 1936

English caravan never went very far, either literally or figuratively. The ones found pottering about the countryside at the beginning of World War I were rounded up and shipped to Calais and made to serve as ambulances at the front. When hostilities ceased in 1918, a few small firms in London and Manchester continued to build them for sale and rent as vacation vehicles, but it certainly never occurred to the proper English that these little two-wheeled cabins, looking so much like truncated railway cabooses, might actually be lived in permanently.

That was strictly an American idea.

Perhaps because England has no Florida, no southern California, no balmy, palmy Camelot where the mildness of the climate might make life in an overgrown cigar box conceivable, the American disease of "trailer fever" never really became epidemic there. To the English, a caravan was simply a camping vehicle, temporary digs for a short holiday in the wilds. And so it remained until the onset of World War II.

But even as a camping vehicle, your typical English caravan of the 1920s was light-years ahead of American design:

> In the first place, these perambulating motor flats are waterproof, steel-armoured, and may be enamelled in any gay colour you like, so that they don't rust; secondly they have tyred wheels, and only two at that, so that they can run along the roughest roads as airily as water wagtails; thirdly, they may be divided into at least three comfortable rooms, all as light as could be with big bungalow windows, and the living-room fitted out with chintz-covered settees, folding writing-desks, book-cases—every conceivable whatnot that a thoroughly educated and up-to-date gipsy . . . could desire. You don't have to rough it in the caravan of 1928; in fact, you can't.

This from the London *Spectator* of July 28, 1928—that same sweltering July in which the future father of the American trailer industry was up in northern Michigan wrestling with wet canvas, about to go home and create an ugly and claustrophobic little six-by-nine wooden box barely tall enough to sit upright in, and peddle it to hundreds of eager midwesterners as the very last word in camping convenience.

Not that Sherman was the first Yank to reinvent the English wheel. By no means. Photos of home-built camp trailers popped up in U.S.

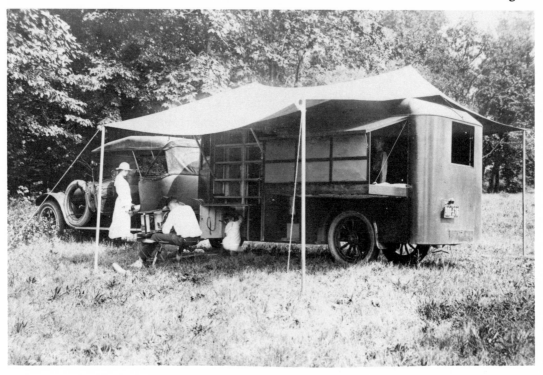

Aviator Glenn Curtiss built this camping trailer in 1917, a fifth-wheeler he called the Motor Bungalow. A clever combination of airplane and boat design, it became the prototype for the house trailers of the thirties and forties. (Photo courtesy the Glenn H. Curtiss Museum, Hammondsport, N.Y.)

newspapers and magazines throughout the teens, invariably created by an evangelist or carpenter or soap salesman to fulfill some private dream: a family odyssey to Texas or California, as often as not. But it was a world-famous aircraft designer who first tried to mass-produce trailers in America—and failed.

Aviation pioneer Glenn Curtiss created his first trailer at least a dozen years before Sherman's little wooden box. Pictures of the "Curtiss Motor Bungalow" in the February 7, 1920, *Scientific American* show a long, sleek plywood lozenge, over six feet high inside, with a flat roof rounded on all four sides giving the vehicle the appearance of an inverted bathtub or a loaf of homemade bread. The Motor Bungalow's wheels are far to the rear, throwing most of the its weight onto the back axle of the towcar through a patented gooseneck hitch, and qualifying it as America's first commercially built "fifth-wheeler." The body is narrow, just under six feet wide, to match the cars and roads of the day, so Curtiss solved his interior space problem with canvas-covered tilt-out beds—two per side—that nearly tripled the vehicle's width. Tent-trailer manufacturers still use this trick today.

But the chief contribution of the Motor Bungalow was its unique structure. Curtiss seems to have been the first to recognize that an automobile trailer is structurally much closer to an airplane than a house. Like an airplane, it needs to be both light enough to fly and strong enough to land in one piece. And so the Bungalow was built of canvas and plywood over a wire-braced skeleton of aircraft spruce, very much like the fuselage structure of the Curtiss "Jenny" biplanes of World War I.

And yet, despite all its innovations, the Motor Bungalow was never a commercial success. People who could afford such a light, sophisticated, aerodynamic vehicle preferred, for reasons all their own, to put their money into the big, square, overweight, four-mile-per-gallon "house-cars" of the day. For some reason, things that run along the highway "as airily as water wagtails" have never appealed much to Americans.

There was, of course, a whole class of people who might have loved the Motor Bungalow, had they been able to afford it: the mobile poor. Day laborers, migratory fruit pickers, seasonal factory workers and the like, these folk were already beginning to tack together homemade trailers and house-cars, setting them in little semipermanent camps around the fringes of America's towns and cities. Detroit had at least one such camp as early as 1920.

But Curtiss wanted nothing to do with such people. He felt—and rightly—that if the poor began to use trailers for homes, it would hurt the trailer's image with the well-to-do. And in Curtiss's book, the well-to-do were the people who counted. So he kept the price of his Motor Bungalow far up in the stratosphere, where only the rich could fly. When he ran out of rich, around 1922, he promptly quit building Motor Bungalows.

For a number of years, Curtiss went back to airplane designing and pushed the trailer idea to a back burner. But there it continued to simmer, refusing to boil dry. A miniature house on wheels, a highway

The Aerocar Land Yacht was the most elegant trailer of the depression era, costing from $3,000 to $25,000. This one has a flying bridge up front, two bathrooms, and servants' quarters in the rear. (Photo courtesy National Automotive History Collection, Detroit Public Library.)

yacht—the idea continued to tantalize Curtiss. There was something fascinating, challenging, *romantic* about the concept of scaling down an apartment, making it light and airy and portable enough to take on the highway. And highways were getting wider and smoother and more inviting every day.

When Curtiss finally reintroduced the Motor Bungalow in 1928, about all that remained of the original design was its bread-loaf roof, its aerodynamic sleekness, and its curious gooseneck hitch. Inside, this new trailer (he renamed it, with deliberate pretension, the "Aerocar Land Yacht") was clearly no camper. It had taken on much of the chromium flash of the finest custom-built house-cars—exceeded them, in fact, by a deliberate harkening back to the styling and elegance of the private Pullman car of the previous century. This new Curtiss trailer had Pullman-style seats, Pullman-style bunks, Pullman-style doors, and Pullman-style windows. It had two and sometimes three complete bathrooms—the smallest in the cook/chauffeur's quarters back in the stern. It had onboard reservoirs of hot and cold running water, and a primitive form of air conditioning that scooped up outside air, filtered it through steel wool, and blew it over dry ice.

The Aerocar Land Yacht. Was it elegant? The entire outside of each and every one was upholstered—tucked and rolled in a rich dark leatherette. Some of the larger models (thirty-foot and up) were even equipped with a "flying bridge," a section of roof at the bow that slid back to reveal padded captain's chairs behind pop-up roadster windshields. To add to the romance, an authentic aircraft instrument panel provided passengers not only with compass headings, but groundspeed and altitude readings as well (Lindbergh was America's hero, remember: the tail-end of the twenties was arguably the most air-crazy era in the country's history). And look: a private telephone linked trailer and towcar, so that the man at the wheel could take his sailing orders directly from the bridge.

Now consider this: every Aerocar Land Yacht had a fully equipped galley that was entirely separate from the living area. What sort of people, in the year 1928, wanted their kitchens separated from their parlors? Not the *New Yorker*'s little old lady from Dubuque, certainly. Separate kitchens appealed, then as now, to that class of folk who don't routinely prepare their own food—the carriage trade.

Since his flight of fancy with the little Motor Bungalow, Curtiss had come solidly back to earth. He had walked in the gardens of the ultrarich and learned something of their tastes. And their tastes, in the days of Calvin Coolidge and bathtub gin, did not run to simplicity. Their tastes ran to chrome-plated elegance, and Curtiss gave it to them in spades. For more than ten years his Land Yachts continued to be the standard of excellence in American trailers, with price tags beginning at three thousand dollars and soaring above fifteen thousand. This in an era when a really nice little eighteen-foot coach that slept four could be had for around eight hundred bucks—loaded, as they say, to the gills.

If the quiet, bespectacled father of the American trailer industry had

"This trailer is strictly in the luxury class, equipped with the finest appointments known to trailering. Not adaptable to the needs of most people. . . ."
—Aerocar press release, *Trailer Topics*, December 1937

ever heard of an English motor caravan—much less a Curtiss Land Yacht—the humble camp trailer that took shape in his Detroit garage that winter of 1928–29 didn't show it. From all evidence, Sherman designed his first trailer strictly from scratch. Only a soapbox could charge him with plagiarism.

In fairness, it ought to be said that the automobiles of 1928 were mostly square and unimaginative affairs themselves, created by setting up four stiff chairs and an engine block and drawing boxes around them. The streamline concept, the idea that wind-tunnel knowledge might profitably be applied to moving objects other than curveballs and flying machines, was still five years in the future. Glenn Curtiss, with his Land Yachts, was flirting with streamlining, but it was not beautiful streamlining. His insistence on rearward wheels and a gooseneck hitch gave the Land Yacht a peculiar, parrot-beaked ugliness all its own.

Still, even by the squarish standards of the day, Sherman's first trailer was plain. A white box, nine by six by five. Rectangular fender cutouts. One small mail-slot window on each side, for cross-ventilation. Two more up front, stacked one over the other to match the bunk beds within. (The lower front window took a beating from flying gravel, and owners soon found they had to tack tacky-looking cardboard over it when they were on the highway.) Only Sherman's roofline had a touch of grace: it was bowed slightly from side to side, to shed water.

You entered this little jewelbox through a large door in the back, a perfectly logical bad idea that every early trailer designer except Curtiss had to invent—and reject—on his own. A moving box, as pilots like Curtiss instinctively knew, creates a powerful vacuum in its wake. This vacuum fills instantly with dust, most of which will find its way through the cracks of any opening whatsoever in the rear of that box, no matter how tightly sealed. About 1933, when trailer builders began moving their doors to the side, as Curtiss had done in his original Motor Bungalow of 1917, the highway dust problem went away like magic, and American trailering took a giant leap in popularity.

You entered through a door in the back, and the first thing you noticed was that, despite the six-foot width of the trailer's body, there wasn't anything like six feet of shoulder room inside. Down either side ran cupboards and iceboxes and stoves and wheel wells and built-in

"The early [trailers] looked like the Toonerville Trolley . . . but they started something that we don't know the half of yet."
—Homer Burch, manager of Sarasota Trailer Park, 1936

furniture and storage bins. Your movements, like those of a train conductor, were pretty much confined to a narrow isle running right down the middle of the coach.

Welcome to trailer life.

A gasoline campstove on your right indicated that you were in the kitchen. Like the rest of the trailer, this "kitchen" was less than five feet high. Very few children enjoy doing all the cooking on a camping trip, and very few adults enjoy preparing a meal on their hands and knees. Clearly, Sherman had a height problem here. To solve it, he designed a drop-floor for the kitchen aisle—meaning all of the aisle behind the trailer's axle, about four feet in length. When you settled into camp, this four-foot section of floor telescoped down and rested on the ground, so the cook stood in a kind of shallow well, giving even a six-footer ample hatroom.

On your left, across the aisle from the stove, was a built-in floor-to-ceiling pantry, the bottom shelf of which was lined with galvanized tin to serve as an icebox—a twenty-five pounder. Iceboxes, you may or may not recall, weren't rated by their food-carrying capacity, which was nil, but by their ice-carrying capacity, often immense. A twenty-five pounder held one block of ice; a fifty-pounder, two. Either model would be swamped by today's buying habits: milk in gallon jugs, mayonnaise by the quart, eggs in flats of eighteen. Fortunately, the icebox reigned during an age of hard times and daily shopping.

Forward from both stove and pantry ran two long, low storage bins, stopping just shy of the bottom bunk, which was built against the front wall of the trailer. The linoleum-clad tops of these storage bins provided bench seating for indoor meals that were served on a folding card table set up—where else?—in the aisle. The lower bunk could also seat a diner or two, provided the top one was first folded out of the way.

Simple. Compact. Functional. So homely it grew on you. And outrageously expensive, as first models always are. Sherman bought all his materials at retail, paid a genuine cabinetmaker to do the assembly, and wound up with almost five hundred dollars in this first trailer. At the time, a brand-new Model A Ford roadster sold for $450, a tudor sedan for just $495.

But his kids loved the little vehicle—loved climbing in and out of it, loved playing house in it when the cabinetmaker wasn't around,

Arthur Sherman's 1930 Covered Wagon camper was a simple box on wheels, built in his garage. It sold so well that, by 1936, he had 1,100 employees working around the clock, producing a thousand house trailers a month. (Photo courtesy the Sherman family.)

loved showing it off to their friends. They called it the "Covered Wagon." This suggests that none of the Sherman kids had ever seen a real covered wagon. Certainly it suggests that none of them had ever looked carefully at an outhouse, or they might have come up with another name altogether. But "Covered Wagon" it was, and Daddy had the name, almost as a joke, stencilled on the side.

In August of '29 the Sherman family towed their little Covered Wagon up to those rainy northern Michigan woods, and—holy mackerel, Kingfish!—the thing was more popular than Amos 'n Andy! Wherever they went, dozens of other campers flocked around it, asking the same questions over and over: What did it cost? Can we look inside? Is it really rain tight? Does that ceiling light work? How does it tow? Where can I get one like it? There was no peace and quiet in the woods that summer for Arthur George Sherman and family. They towed their Covered Wagon home.

And on the way home, Daddy got an idea.

That fall, he had a couple more of these curious little Covered Wagons built, one for a friend and the second one "on spec," as contractors say. He thought he'd display it at the Detroit Auto Show the following January, just to see if any of those folk who had driven him out of the woods would show up with cash in their pockets. By judicious buying, and streamlining the building process a bit, he managed to whittle the

Mary and Arthur Sherman (left) entertain friends in their first Covered Wagon. "Trailer tappers" pestered them everywhere they went, causing Sherman to try marketing his little creation. (Photo courtesy the Detroit Historical Department.)

price down to just under four hundred dollars, including a modest profit margin. At such a figure—still perilously close to the cost of a new car—would the Covered Wagon sell?

It did—on the first morning of the show. After which Sherman began taking orders for more—a hundred and seventeen more, all told. Suddenly this trailer thing began to look like it might outgrow the family garage, might even get to be a full-fledged business on its own. The auto show crowds didn't exactly mob the Covered Wagon display, but the people who were interested were *fanatically* interested—asked dozens of questions, crawled all over the show trailer, took measurements, nodded their heads a lot. Some were obviously just do-it-yourselfers, planning to go right home and tack together something like it. But others would come back later to put their names on the waiting list.

And then the old man with the big moustache showed up.

He didn't say much, this old man. He kept his lips clamped around a briar pipe and his thumbs hooked behind a pair of old-fashioned red galluses. But his dark eyes, darting about in the shadow of his hat brim, took in the things that counted. The hitch. The wheels and axles. The springs. The way the body of the trailer was bolted to the frame. He was a quiet one, this old man. You couldn't tell if he was satisfied with what he saw or not.

Finally he turned to the designer. "You TCT?" he asked.

TCT? Sherman thought this might be some sort of union. He was no Henry Ford, but he had enough Henry Ford in him not to care much for labor unions. He shook his head.

"Well, you oughta be. You wanna sell these things, forget about auto shows. You wanna sell these things, join the Tin Can Tourists. Git yerself down to convention."

Then the old man went away.

2 The Tin Canners

To own an automobile is apparently every man's ambition. Having acquired one, he wants to travel, usually as far as he can go.

"On the Road to Elsewhere,"
The Saturday Evening Post, *September 15, 1923*

Indeed, motor-camping is the only way in which many people can afford to travel at all.

—Elon Jessup,
The Motor-Camping Book *(1921)*

For it might, indeed, be difficult to determine whether trailers have developed because of the Tin Can Tourists, or whether the T.C.T., as they are commonly called, have grown with the trailer.

—Freeman Marsh,
Trailers *(1937)*

The Tin Can Tourists of America. The tin canners. The motor gypsies. When Arthur Sherman dragged his poky little six by nine box, his "Covered Wagon," to the 1930 auto show in Detroit, the tin canners had already been around for more than a decade. Around where? Everywhere. Well, everywhere east of the Mississippi, at least. In their tents and bedrolls, these hardy adventurers summered in what they called "the North," meaning the upper Midwest: up on the lake in Wisconsin; or under the tall, shady oaks outside of Sandusky; or down on the water's edge at Orchard Beach State Park, just above Manistee, Michigan.

They wintered on the broad, white beaches of Florida: Bradenton, Clearwater, Sarasota, Tampa. Especially Tampa. They had a thing for

Tin can tourists camped at DeSoto Park, Tampa, on Christmas day, 1920. The Yankees and midwesterners who came south with their tents and trailers and house-cars paved the way for the house trailer revolution of the mid-thirties. (Photo courtesy of Florida State Archives.)

Tampa. It was in East Tampa, out in Desoto Park during the winter of 1919, that the Tin Canners—with capital letters—officially began.

Long before World War I, and long before the advent of national weather reports, rumors of Florida's winter climate crept northward to haunt the snowbound Yankee:

"Heard it was eighty-two degrees one day last week down in Miami."

"Hell you say! What is it out there now?"

"Can't see for the frost on the window . . . looks like eight below."

"Huh! If we was Rocky-fellers, I reckon we'd be in Miami."

And of course they were in Miami—the Rocky-fellers, that is. They slipped away just after Christmas, by steam yacht, by ocean liner, by "private varnish," those exotic and hand-crafted Pullman cars of the very rich, long and sleek and servant-encrusted, with discreetly drawn shades and names like "Pilgrim" and "Idlehour" printed in gilt letters on their forest-green sides. Cars that were coupled quietly and unobtrusively to the rear of southbound express trains just as they were leaving the station.

They arrived with little fanfare, these Rocky-fellers. They stayed at Florida's best hotels, they ate shrimp bernaise and oysters Rockefeller in her most elegant restaurants. They played golf and tennis at her swankiest spas. And then, tanned and rejuvenated, they melted away again in April or May, to return to their money factories in the North. The state of Florida had been invented by the rich for the rich, and in the three decades prior to World War I, the rich had their new invention pretty much to themselves.

Then came the motorcar—in vast numbers. In 1910, America had fewer than half a million automobiles; ten years later the figure had risen to something over eight million—one vehicle for every dozen citizens: man, woman, and child. Tall and gawky and fragile and cantankerous they were, but what a piece of unthinkable magic! What a machine for annihilating distance! To own one was to own seven-league boots . . . to have wings on your heels . . . to hold the reins of Pegasus. Who could hold the reins of Pegasus without craving to go for a ride?

And ride they did. On weekends, on holidays, on vacations, this daring and dust-covered generation of postwar Americans ventured out further and further in their rickety machines, bouncing along two-hundred-year-old wagon ruts, popping and wheezing down hopelessly muddy lanes, fording creeks in creaking Fords, and getting further from home on a casual Sunday afternoon drive than their parents had gone for their honeymoon.

"Heard it was eighty-two degrees one day last week down in Miami."

"Hell you say—let's go give her a look-see. . . ."

Suddenly the states below the snowline found themselves host to a whole new class of winter tourist, more numerous and less quiet than the folk who had come by yacht and private pullman. More numerous and less quiet—and nowhere near as rich.

These new tourists didn't come south to stay at the fancy hotels and resorts, and they didn't come to eat shrimp bernaise and oysters Rockefeller in the elegant restaurants. They came popping and wheezing down U.S. Highway One with tents tied to their muddy running boards, with pots and pans and gasoline campstoves piled in the back seat; pots and pans and gasoline campstoves, and folding chairs and collapsible cots and inflatable mattresses and forty-pound boxes of dirt containing live fishing worms. Never having been so far from their own kitchens, and unsure of what to expect in the way of provisions on the road, they loaded their Fords and Moons and Dodges and battered old Franklin touring cars with canned meat and canned vegetables and even canned fruit—*they brought their own fruit to Florida*. The great American motor-camping craze had begun.

It didn't take long for the locals to size up these new visitors, to get them stereotyped to satisfaction:

"I s'pose you heard about th' Yankee that come south fer th' winter with one clean shirt an' a ten-dollar bill, an' never changed neither one. . . ."

"They drive tin cans and they eat outa tin cans and they leave a trail of tin cans behind 'em. They're tin-can tourists, that's what they are."

Tin can tourists. The label wasn't particularly fair, for the cars and the eating habits of these nouveau gypsies were, on the whole, no tinnier than anyone else's. But the phrase had a nasty ring to it, and it stuck. It appealed especially to real estate salesmen and hotel keepers and restaurant owners, all of whom were heartily sick of seeing carloads of these strangers go gawking and pointing past their door, in search of a stretch of open beach, a vacant lot, an unfenced schoolyard to pound their tent stakes into for the night.

"Just lookit them fools! Don't they know that all that land out there belongs to somebody? They're just freeloaders, ever one of 'em— nothin' but a buncha damn tin canners!"

Now condescension of this sort is cheap and easy, and it can be a great comfort to the condescender. But it takes two to play the game. What happens if the object of your scorn doesn't care a whit for your opinion? Suppose he refuses to see himself as your inferior—just laughs at your sneers, makes a joke of the names you call him?

And that's exactly what those damned infuriating Yankees did. Those *tin can tourists* in their stinking, noisy, overloaded, mud-covered flivvers simply refused to be intimidated. In their hearts and in their tents they knew they were the social equals of the realtors and hotel keepers and restaurant owners who derided them—if for no other reason, because so many of them were themselves realtors and hotel and restaurant owners back home. They weren't gypsies and they weren't freeloaders, and they knew it. They were substantial middle-class Americans (maybe even a cut above average—hell's bells, they owned motorcars, didn't they?) who were out looking for a change of scenery and a breath of fresh air and a little adventure and good fellowship under the stars. Why, dammit, they were motor campers! Didn't those crazy crackers read *Popular Science* and *The Saturday Evening Post*? Didn't they know there was a fad going on?

And so, when it came time to organize all this adventure and good fellowship, to create for themselves a kind of Elks lodge of the open road, the motor campers had no trouble choosing a name for their club. They would be the Tin Can Tourists of America—the TCT.

Their founder was a genial chap from Chicago named James M. Morrison. A veteran motor camper himself, Morrison planted the idea for the club among some twenty-two families camped in Tampa's De Soto Park in December of 1919. Within two months they were chartered; an organization with "no fees, no dues, no graft," whose motto was the Golden Rule. If Morrison and his fellow-founders had any social or political aims—to fight for better highways, say, or more government campgrounds, or fewer signs in schoolyards that said "no tourists allowed"—these aims were conspicuously absent from the club charter, which merely hoped

> to unite fraternally all auto campers; to establish a feeling of friendship among them and a friendly basis with local residents; to provide clean and wholesome entertainment in camps and at meetings; to spread the gospel of cleanliness in all camps, as well as enforce rules governing all camp grounds; to put out all campfires, destroy no property, and purloin nothing; to help a fellow member in distress on the road without injury to one's self or car.

And how was one to recognize fellow members in distress on the road? Simple; their cars would be displaying the proud badge of the

TCT, an empty soup can dangling from the radiator cap. Total strangers, sailing past one another with cans at full mast, would hail each other like brothers. Often they'd heave to and trade road information, using license plates in lieu of names: "Say there, New York—how much farther to Steubenville?" When they parted, still without exchanging names, it was with a hearty "seeya at convention!" The Tin Can Tourists.

Their winter convention was in Tampa, usually in late January or early February. Summer Convention, in August, would be in some cool, shady spot "up north." The main business of Winter Convention was to decide when and where Summer Convention was to be held, and vice versa. And to vote in a new "Royal Can Opener"—their chief executive officer—for the coming year, and announce the winner of the day's horseshoe tournament, while speculating on how the shoes might fall for the various players the next day. Then might come a few rousing group songs, including three or four repetitions of the official theme song of the TCT:

> The more we get together,
>   Together, together,
> The more we get together,
> The happier we'll be.
>   For your friends are my friends
>   And my friends are your friends,
> The more we get together,
>   The happier we'll be.

The tin canners. They went popping and wheezing and tenting and singing their merry way right through the Roaring Twenties, making converts left and right, for every member was empowered to swear in new Canners on the spot, wherever their trails might cross—no fees, no dues, no graft—and invite them to the next convention. Within a decade TCT membership had grown to almost 100 thousand—estimated, of course, because no one kept written records.

The tin canners. Hadn't they read Sinclair Lewis, Hemingway, Scott Fitzgerald? Weren't they aware that they were glad handing their way right through the Jazz Age, the Age of Cynicism? Did they have any idea what scorn H. L. Mencken would have heaped on their innocent and homely little boy scout charter, their secret handshake (a sawing motion), secret sign (a "C" made with the thumb and forefinger), or secret password ("nit nac")? Did they stop to think of what the sharp-tongued Dorothy Parker might have made of a group of adults—total strangers for the most part—crouched about a campfire in shirt-sleeves, popping their old-fashioned galluses and singing

The more we get together,
Together, together. . . .

Did they care? For every Sinclair Lewis there are probably a thousand Babbits—a ratio that seems to work out about right for everybody involved.

The tin canners. Like most Americans, like most people, they disliked the continual change they saw going on all around them. They were suspicious of all this progress, progress, progress. They idealized the past and looked with suspicion upon the future. The past, in their minds, was simple and easygoing and folksy—Arcadian. The past was the golden age of friendliness and camaraderie among strong, free, independent, self-sufficient people. The past was classless and democratic. And most of all, the past was rural.

This was their myth, their dream, their Holy Grail. Every summer they went out on the highway in search of it. They packed their bedrolls and cranked up their Tin Lizzies and puttered off looking for the past. And—as so often happens—what they found instead was the future. For the Tin Can Tourists of the twenties, with their auto camps and their sweet dream of Arcady, quite literally paved the way for the house trailer revolution of the following decade.

"A census last Sunday on the Daniel Webster Highway at Laconia [New Hampshire] disclosed that 20 per cent of passenger automobiles, exclusive of local about-town motors, were equipped with camping paraphernalia."
—*The Christian Science Monitor,*
Aug. 19, 1924

The tin canners. They were actually only a small part—a sample, a kind of midwestern cross-section—of the whole motor-camping picture. At the peak of the movement, during the late twenties, the American Automobile Association estimated that between ten and twelve million U.S. motorists were hitting the road each summer with their tents and cookstoves.

Not all these wanderers stayed in TCT territory, east of the Mississippi. Many went west, into the treeless wilderness "beyond Omaha," out into the Kingdom of Dust, where American motor camping had gotten its start, not as a sport but as a necessity. Out beyond Omaha, the towns were just like the trees: low and spare, and few and far between. "Automobilists" who crossed the western plains and deserts—and they'd been doing so with dogged regularity ever since the summer of 1903—had to be prepared to eat and sleep wherever night found them. A hotel was a rare luxury, and privately operated tourist homes and cabins, of the sort that were beginning to spring up in vacation spots and along the heavily travelled routes of the east, were still almost unknown on the western prairies and deserts.

Much to their surprise, however, the early motor campers who ventured west found a warmer welcome in many of the plains towns than they were accustomed to receiving in the villages of the east and south, for they happened to arrive at just the right moment in history to fall heir to a dying tradition, a tradition largely unknown back East: the municipal wagon yard.

Farmers and ranchers in the West were used to driving fifty to a hundred miles, by horse and wagon, to buy provisions in the nearest town—a two- or three-day trip, in good weather. When they arrived, they needed some place to unhitch and feed and water their teams. Town merchants found it good business to set aside such an area for their use: a square block or so at the edge of the business district, with a few trees for shade, a little grass for the horses. Not every rancher who made the long trek into town could afford to patronize the local hotel; many slept in or under their wagons, cooking their meals on open fires right in the wagon yard.

So it was only natural that, when the first auto-campers chugged into town after World War I, they were directed to make themselves at home "down to the wagon yard." And they did, driving their tent stakes into the sunbaked prairie right alongside the horse-drawn rigs of tanned and weathered and slow-talking cowboys—a breed of men they thought existed only in dime novels. Here was one of those rare junctures of history: the pioneers of two radically different ages, the solid citizens of two distinct Americas, camped cheek by jowl and swapping stories over a common campfire.

As the twenties wore on, the wagons became fewer and the motorcars more numerous. People took to calling the wagon yard the "auto camp," and the town fathers saw fit to add a few amenities—some

"The most conspicuous thing in the West now is the sign, Free Municipal Camp Ground. Almost every city, town, and hamlet, from the Dakotas to the Pacific, maintains such a campground, and it is in constant use."
—*The Nation,*
September 14, 1924

picnic tables, an acre or so of cropped grass, a separate privy for the womenfolk—to make the place a bit more attractive to the growing stream of easterners so obviously hell-bent on seeing America through a dusty windshield—"Comin' clear out here," as one Kansan put it in 1923, "just to inhale our topsoil." By 1930, every western town worth its salt had an auto camp, and the term "wagon yard" had passed out of the language.

Those campers from the East who ventured out onto the plains during the teens and early twenties took the wagon yard idea home with them: a little public campground just for tourists, out near the edge of town, but still convenient to the local gas station and cafe and grocery and dry goods store. You didn't have to be an economics professor to see the value of the tourist dollar, the dollar that was earned elsewhere and spent in your town by people who were just passing through. Unlike the permanent citizenry, these motor campers required little in the way of expensive civic services such as police and fire protection, garbage collection and sewerage. They were easy to please. Just give them a couple of acres of tamed nature—a few shade trees with some short grass and a low snake count—and they'd rattle off down the highway praising your town to everybody they met:

"Say there, New York—how much farther to Steubenville?"

"Well, it's a long twelve miles, Michigan, but worth it. They got this free campground on a little creek just south of town. Really first class. Me and the missus spent two extra days there—friendliest doggone people you ever met. Try Elma's Cafe on Main Street, if you like steaks!"

"Much oblige there, New York—seeya at convention!"

Meanwhile, the federal government, in addition to helping the states put together a highway system, had begun to take note of all those tents and cots on the running boards and set to work building motor campgrounds in the national forests and national parks. Washington, D.C., set the standard for the entire East Coast with its thousand-car motor camp out under the big lombardy poplars in East Potomac Park; twenty-two thousand tenters checked into this camp during the summer of 1924 alone.

Nor was private enterprise far behind. People who happened to own one of those small tracts of tamed nature—especially one that fronted on some main tourist route—found the free municipal campgrounds

easy to compete with. Just raise the ante by a single amenity—put in
some showerbaths, say, or a special area to wash the dust off your
Ford—and you'd soon have more business than you could handle,
even at seventy-five cents to a dollar a night per car. These motor
campers, it appeared, weren't broke—give them something worth paying for and just watch 'em shell out for it.

"Coolidge prosperity" had come to America. And the Coolidge prosperity of the middle and late twenties wasn't confined merely to the
great stock manipulators, or even the great Gatsbys; it was beginning
to seep down to the common folk, those folk who went touring by
tent and car: the motor-gypsies, the "roadsiders," the tin can tourists.

As the decade wore on, you could see the effects of this prosperity
in the camps and conventions and reunions of the TCT. More and
more canners, it seemed, were getting too good—or was it merely too
old?—to sleep night after night on a folding cot, under a piece of loose
canvas angled down from the roof of the car. More and more of them
were sporting fancy new umbrella tents, or one of those slick tent-
trailer contraptions with innerspring mattresses—and shiny new cars
with closed tops, too, so their hairdos wouldn't get mussed en route.
More and more of them were starting to worry about appearances,
about shoeshines and shirttails and such.

Hell, just say it: a lot of tin canners were getting stuck up. The
problem was, by the late twenties, the "white-pants Willies" were beginning to take over the club. Hadn't they already voted to change the
name to Tin Can Tourists of the *World*? And issued celluloid lapel
buttons for people to wear at Convention? And started referring to the
Royal Can Opener as the Royal *Chief*? And dropped the old soup can
on the radiator cap in favor of a fancy new diamond-shaped radiator
emblem you had to pay 50¢ for!

"Some people just gettin' too good for their own good—next thing
you know, they'll be after changin' the club's name! Why, sooner
change the name of Kalamazoo!"

And if you raised a fuss about any of this high hat foolishness, they'd
label you a bolshevik and send you off to camp in the Tin Lizzie
section—no matter what kind of car you were driving.

By the end of the decade, by that fateful day on Wall Street when

By the middle twenties, the once-despised tin canners were being courted for their tourist dollars by almost every town and village in Florida. Typical was this municipal camp at Gainesville. (Photo courtesy Florida State Archives.)

the great frail bubble of the Roaring Twenties finally burst, auto-camping was no longer just a fad—it was an industry. Hundreds of companies were busy supplying not only cookstoves and tents and elaborate tent-trailers like the one that frustrated Arthur Sherman, but folding cots and chairs and tables and spoons; collapsible baby cribs and bathtubs; magic boxes small enough to bolt to your car's running board but large enough to contain a picnic service for six, complete with table and awning. The 1920s was the first golden age of American gadgetry, when virtually everything that might make life on Madison Avenue worth living was invented, and perfected, and made available to all—including the word "gadget" itself.

The effect of all of this money changing was to raise the status of the lowly sport of auto-camping, to make it respectable—even in the eyes of those southern realtors and hotel keepers and restaurant owners who had screamed the loudest when the fad began. Suddenly the TCT, despite their homely name, found they were no longer outsiders, undesirables. Suddenly they were being courted by every aggressive small town chamber of commerce in the state of Florida: Come to Arcadia for Homecoming Week! Don't miss the big Thanksgiving Party at Winter Haven! Plan now to attend the TCT Reunion in Lake City! Other states quickly followed suit, and by the time the market collapsed in October of '29, the tin can tourists—with or without capital letters—could find a warm welcome and a cool place to pitch their tents in almost every hamlet in America.

And then came the Great Depression.

People whose business it was to chart the effects of the crash—economists, financial advisers, news analysts—continued to predict a rosy future for auto-camping, despite the plummeting price of stocks, the cooling smokestacks, the growing breadlines in the cities. Oh, some of the suppliers of the more esoteric gadgetry (New! Chromium-plated Folding Auto Vanity, only $24 postpaid!) might see some shrinkage in their market. But on the whole, the prophets declared, the motor camping industry was sound, and likely to continue growing.

Wasn't it grounded, after all, on the bedrock of Spartanism? Cooking over an open fire, sleeping under the stars, seeing the country "on the cheap"? Surely such pure and wholesome activities could not fail to soothe the righteous wrath of the gods—those gods who seemed bent on punishing an entire nation for the hubris of the hundred wealthy financiers, fifty mafiosa, five novelists, and one overrated cartoonist named John Held, Jr., who were—as everybody knew—responsible for most of the excesses of the Jazz Age.

Surely, at a time when elegant hotels and spiffy restaurants were collapsing like umbrella tents, when the private Pullman cars of the formerly rich were being turned into roadside diners—surely at such a time the humble motor-camping industry could expect, if not to inherit the earth, at least to see a lot of new faces at the retail counter.

And yet, by 1932—the year the country hit rock bottom, the year the price of wheat fell to its lowest figure in three centuries—the sport and industry of motor camping was as dead as Warren G. Harding.

Where did they go, those legions of tanned and hardy partisans of fresh air and sunshine, those twelve million part-time gypsies? What made them fold their tents like Longfellow's Arabs and silently steal (purloining nothing) away?

They were faddists, of course, all but the hard core of them—faddists in a country that had been swept by fads before, and would be again. Mah-jongg, pedal cars, Florida real estate, bobbed hair, flagpole sitting, marathon dancing, miniature golf: all brave new fads that had come and gone during the fifteen or so years of the auto-camping craze.

But to label something a fad is merely to categorize it, not to explain it; to answer the *what* but not the *why*. Why did ten to twenty million Americans—nearly a fifth of the nation—participate in this one particular fad, this sport of motor camping? What was its appeal? What made it so irresistible to so many for so long?

Car camping in the teens and twenties was a happy combination of two powerful strains of American romanticism: back to nature and the song of the open road. The spidery little motorcars of that era were much closer in spirit to a modern motorcycle than a modern automobile, and a motor vacation back then was something more akin to a motorcycle trip today—a motorcycle trip over dirt roads, on an old and fragile and unreliable machine with very bad tires. Even the most expensive cars of the twenties—the Lincolns and Auburns, the Dusenbergs and Marmons—were not nearly as insulated and padded and soundproofed and airtight as the sleek, sealed caskets that whine along our interstates now.

> "Fascinating and romantic were the tales of the nomadic gypsies who had no settled homes, but camped each night somewhere along the roadside or in the heart of the forest."
> —Opening sentence of auto-camping article, *Review of Reviews,* May 1921

In 1925, when you went motoring in the desert, you breathed the thick, cottony desert air, and you felt the slip and crunch of the hot sand under your wheels. Every time a tire blew you knelt in that hot sand to patch it, and the sand got in your shoes and your pants cuffs and your tool bag and your eyes, so that years later—long after the sunset hues of the Grand Canyon, the salt air of the Pacific had faded from your memory—that hot desert sand would remain vivid in your mind. And when the desert erupted into mountains, you shifted down, and down again, and climbed them slowly, painfully, foot by hard-earned foot, and the air that streamed in around the windshield turned cool and fine, and you smelled every change in elevation, from the sage to the juniper to the tall Douglas fir and the massive Ponderosa with its sweet brown bark like alligator hide. Driving through the mountains, your body registered each harsh thump of granite beneath the tires, and long before evening you knew those mountains in your bones. The motorists of the teens and twenties did not simply see America, they *experienced* it—land and climate and people—in a manner long since closed to everyone but a few cross-country bicyclists and motor-cyclists.

Back to nature. The song of the open road. Listen to Elon Jessup, author of *The Motor–Camping Book* (Putnam, 1921), writing in a for-gotten magazine called *Outlook* about a seven-thousand-mile auto trip he and his family took in the summer of '23:

> We have found that by pitching a tent each night and cooking our own meals we can travel great distances by car for a comparatively small amount of money; also be surprisingly comfortable and receive greater insight and more real value than in most other methods of travel. . . . We were free agents who could stay as long as we liked, come and go as we pleased. . . . It's a great country—really great. I never knew so before. I've become quite mad about it. The beauty, variety, and people.

Back to nature. The song of the open road. But not without a tinge of guilt, for Jessup is quick to add:

> Perhaps some motor campers are taking longer vacations than the wheels of progress ordinarily countenance. But if progress insists on building its cities topheavy it must expect something of a reaction.

The 1920s witnessed the passionate beginning of our national love affair with the automobile, that magic carpet mankind had been dream-ing of for centuries. By the time of Jessup's trip, the cheap, mass-produced American motorcar had already made an entire generation—and their sons and daughters—free agents who could come and go as they pleased. It had already created a new institution, the Sunday after-noon family drive into the country—a ritual weekly escape out of America's "topheavy" cities and back to Grandma's farm.

So what could be more natural than to extend this escape, at vacation time, into a camping expedition into the great outdoors—a weeks-long quest for that elusive and ever-retreating Nature that poets and jour-nalists sing of? Twenty million American families possessed a magic carpet, a time machine that could whisk them back to the Garden of Eden. Who could leave such a machine in the garage all summer?

And yet, by 1932, all the magic had gone out of motor camping. Where did it go? How did the Depression manage to kill such an innocent, healthful, inexpensive family recreation as tenting on the old camp ground?

The culprit was not the house trailer. By 1932 Arthur Sherman had been joined by a couple of dozen other manufacturers turning out these curious, crude, overpriced little flying flats—but turning them out one at a time, in their spare time, in garages, barns, and back yards, and selling them mostly to neighbors and friends and relatives and an occasional perfect stranger who happened to see the one Uncle Buck and Aunt Minnie had and wanted something like it. Sherman's Covered Wagon Company, not yet incorporated but already the largest trailer manufacturer in America, sold a grand total of eighty units in 1932; only 189 in 1933. No, the infant trailer industry, in the early thirties, was hardly a threat to America's tentmakers—or anyone else.

The culprit, as fate would have it, was the canvas tent itself.

In the bull market summer of '29, the summer Arthur Sherman took to the woods in his first Covered Wagon, the tent was still the symbol of the fresh-air-and-sunshine crowd, the legions of healthy, wholesome, undebauched sojourners in Nature: the gasoline gypsies, the tin canners. But the winter of 1929–30, following the October crash, saw some three million middle- and low-income Americans thrown out of work as business and industry tightened their belts and prepared to ride out the economic storm. Soon individuals too began to economize. Even people not directly touched by the events on Wall Street, where thirty billion dollars had evaporated into thin air in less than a month, smelled fear. "Reckon it won't hurt to cut back the galavantin' for one summer—things'll perk up next year. We'll sit tight awhile, an' then we'll take us a real camping trip, come the summer of '31."

But of course things didn't perk up. Come the summer of '31 there was a brand-new word in the American vocabulary, an ugly and frightening word, and it seemed to be on everybody's lips. The word was "Hooverville."

A Hooverville was a shantytown, a rag-tag camp, out by the city dump, usually, and full of the *nouveau poor*: decent, law-abiding families, mostly, who had lost jobs, homes, status, hope—lost everything, it seemed, but their rattletrap car—and found themselves in makeshift huts, huddled together out at the edge of the town's consciousness, living on handouts, odd jobs, charity, "the dole." Not every town had its Hooverville, but almost every consciousness did. It was right there in a dark corner of the mind, whispering over and over, "One piece of bad luck, one slip on the economic ladder, and you could be right down here with us." To say that the Great Depression broke the spirit of an entire generation is hardly an exaggeration.

And to say that Hoovervilles killed the great American tent-camping fad is no exaggeration, either, for a person couldn't help but notice that in any given Hooverville, about half the folk there were living in tents. When they were on the move—and it seemed like they were constantly on the move, looking for work, looking for a friendly face, looking for a warm south wind—they carried their few pathetic possessions with them, strapped to the roofs and running boards of their battered, mud-encrusted old cars and looking for all the world like a bunch of . . . motor campers.

It can be argued, I suppose, that the great auto-camping fraternity of the twenties was the salt of the earth, friendly and unpretentious and democratic to a fault. It can be argued that they were the last folk you would accuse of snobbery—the very last people to care a hoot if strangers mistook them for down-and-outers, for migrants, for auto tramps. . . .

> For your friends are my friends
> And my friends are your friends. . . .

It can be argued that most of the tin canners—like many of the barons of Wall Street—simply ran out of money and had to give up their summer sojourning up around the Lakes, their winter trips to Florida and California and south Texas, had to stay home by the millions and tend to the garden, paint the trim on the house, peddle leather ties to the neighbors, make fabulous profits raising giant mushrooms in the cellar.

It can be argued that the image of poverty that the canvas tent and the running-board bedroll acquired almost overnight after the crash of

'29 had little or nothing to do with the demise of auto-camping, a fad that had just about run its course anyway.

Be that as it may, the mass market for tents and tent-trailers simply evaporated by 1932 and didn't reappear until the middle fifties, when a whole new generation—a generation that knew the word "Hooverville" mostly from history books—suddenly discovered that auto-camping their way through America's state and national parks was a great way to get the family "back to nature"—while singing, in their airconditioned Chevys, the song of the open road.

3 From Camping to Living

At first . . . the trailer was just something different in camping. Then people discovered you could live in them.

—Fortune,
March 1937

The trailer is a hybrid of the aeroplane, automobile and house in construction and engineering.

—Trailer Topics,
June 1940

All things exist in a state of perpetual change.

—Heraclitus

With the tent and bedroll in eclipse, what was the hardcore motor camper, the person who had survived the Crash with wanderlust intact, supposed to do? Give up sleeping under the stars? And what was to happen to the Tin Can Tourists themselves, now a hundred-thousand strong, with their ten-year tradition of conventions and homecomings and holiday get-togethers all over southern Florida? Were these hardy and courageous old wanderers, after thumbing their noses at public opinion for over a decade, going to be forced (by social pressure, of all things!) to turn respectable at last?

The posh city hotel and the dingy rural bungalow camp beckoned to them from opposite ends of the economic spectrum. But neither hotel nor bungalow touring was anything like camping out—being on your own, blazing new trails, pulling off the road wherever evening found you. The elements of freedom and self-sufficiency were missing. True, by traveling the hotel or bungalow routes, you were still seeing the country. You were out there on the open road, gobbling up the miles. But it was hardly what you could call back to nature: sleeping in other people's beds, dancing to their tune, and paying them good money for the privilege. It was entirely too predictable, too structured, too mundane a way to go touring. It was camping in, not camping out. And the old campfire camaraderie was missing, too. Racing from hotel to hotel, from cabin to cabin, simply wasn't romantic, wasn't a pioneer experience.

Into this dilemma stepped—fell, actually—our bacteriologist from Detroit, Arthur George Sherman and his six by nine wooden box on wheels, his Covered Wagon. Never in the history of American gadgetry has there been a man so exactly in the right place with the right idea at the right time.

For Detroit was the hub of the Great Lakes states: those rolling green heartlands that turn so gray and soggy and miserably cold toward the middle of December, the home states of a good 80 percent of the Florida-bound auto-campers of the twenties. Detroit was the hub, too, of the automobile industry, a handy place to shop for springs and axles and wheels and tires, if you happened to need such things. And, as luck would have it, the auto industry in 1929 was just getting out of the wood business—just starting to phase out oak frame-members and polished wood dashboards—when Sherman began to build his wooden trailers. What better time to be in the market for wood—and wood-workers?

By 1933, Sherman's little garage operation had outgrown the family garage and begun a series of expansions that would culminate, two years later, in a 150,000-square-foot plant in the suburban village of Mount Clemens. Sherman had begun a sporadic ad campaign in *National Geographic* and *Field and Stream* back in 1931, and it seemed at last to be paying off: every year more and more people came looking for a Covered Wagon. But his main source of customers was still the grapevine of the hard-core autocampers, for Sherman had by now found out that "TCT" didn't stand for some labor union:

"Hey, Michigan, where'd you get that trailer rig?"

"Up in Detroit! Bought her right outa the front yard of Sherman

Homemade trailers like this Texas rig outnumbered factory models by two to one until around 1936. Heavy and poorly designed, they helped prejudice public opinion against the trailer.

Laboratories, out on Jefferson Avenue. Had three, four of 'em just sittin' there under the trees. Lady that sold me was Mrs. Sherman herself, the millionaire's wife, can you believe it?"

"Sherman Laboratories on Jefferson. Thanks for the info, Michigan— seeya at convention!"

By 1933, of course, Sherman was not alone in the trailer business. Even before the economy bottomed out in late '32, the trailer industry had begun growing quietly—so quietly that hardly anyone recognized it as an industry at all. In garages, in back yards, in machine shops and cabinet works all over America, people were busy assembling little cabin-boxes from mail-order plans and parts, assembling them and mounting them on junkyard wheels and axles with dead names on their hubcaps: Essex, Moon, Peerless, Simplex, Willys-Knight.

Quiet people, mostly, these trailer makers—not unlike Arthur Sherman himself: tinkerers, putterers, dreamers, close scrutinizers of *Pop-*

ular Mechanics. In those inch-high ads that jammed the back pages of *PM* and *Modern Mechanix* and *Popular Science Monthly,* a dozen trailer supply firms hawked their curious wares: hitches, drop axles, sinks, windows, dome lights, ventilators, cabinet latches—all the specialized hardware you needed to

> Build your own Camp Trailer in your spare time! No experience necessary! Send today for our Free Plans Book and Catalogue. . . .

No experience necessary. Thousands of enthusiastic but untalented people took these words on faith—and their handiwork showed it. The roadside ditches of the early thirties were littered with the bones of pathetic homemade wheeled contraptions that had failed their road tests. In December of 1936, *Business Week* estimated the number of homebuilts on the road at 100,000, remarking that "many of these trailers are unsafe and an eyesore, and probably help prejudice public opinion against trailers generally."

Not every homebuilt trailer looked as if it had been assembled and painted by torchlight, of course. Some of them were rolling displays of their builders' skill and creativity, trig little doll houses that caused friends and neighbors and even total strangers to exclaim, "What would you charge to build me one like that?" And that's how most of the thirties trailer manufacturers got their start: build the first one for yourself, then one for sale, then another. It was a road Arthur Sherman knew well—he'd been down it with a Covered Wagon.

How many of these back yard builders turned professional? A staggering number. The *National Used Car Market Report,* in a special trailer edition published in the fall of 1936, listed all the models offered by the top one hundred manufacturers, plus the names and addresses of no less than seven hundred other known commercial builders. At the beginning of that same year *Sunset* magazine found eighty-five trailer makers in Los Angeles alone.

In the early days of the automobile, every town and village in America had its side street garage—red brick walls, tin roof, the air inside cool and musty as a mineshaft—that turned out two, five, maybe ten more or less identical vehicles a year, on demand, with the town's name stamped proudly on front and rear. So it was with the house trailers of the thirties. Among my oldest friends is a Texas couple, E. L.

"Some say [the trailer] is a product of the depression, and hence merely an emergency device to escape the tax collector and the landlord."
—*Christian Science Monitor,* October 7, 1936

and Ella Mae James, who were married in '37 and moved into a small trailer built by an enterprising blacksmith in the central Texas town of Cross Plains. E. L. was a contractor, and he paid for their little honeymoon castle—in which two of their three children were born—by putting a rock veneer on the blacksmith's house.

Was that blacksmith in Cross Plains listed among the eight hundred trailer builders in the *National Used Car Market Report*? Not likely. Estimates of the actual number of firms that built and sold house trailers between 1930 and 1940 ran as high as two thousand—a nice round figure, and probably conservative.

The surprising thing is, as late as 1935 these two thousand trailer builders barely knew of each other's existence—or cared. Business was good: the number of orders coming in the front door always stayed slightly ahead of the number of trailers going out the back. Times were hard, so skilled labor was both plentiful and cheap. Few of these fledgling companies advertised or sought publicity—word of mouth was enough to keep business growing at a slow but comfortable rate. In the early years of the house trailer industry, as in many other Depression industries, caution was the watchword: "We got a good thing going here; no need to shout about it. No need to rock the boat. Remember, we're eating three squares, where a lot of people ain't. Just work hard and keep your head down and don't do nothing to irritate anybody."

"Of course we didn't think of ourselves as pioneers in those days—we were too busy just trying to make a living."
—Joseph Flora of Trotwood Trailers, in conversation, March 1988

For America's "trailermen," as these new entrepreneurs were called, those shaky, tentative years before 1935 were a period of quiet experimentation, of gradual evolution. There were few rules. Each builder was busy discovering, independently, what customers wanted in their camping trailer. And what customers wanted was exactly what old Samuel Gompers of the AF of L wanted: more. More room inside—more headroom, more storage room, more eating room, more sleeping room, more living room.

And more conveniences—more modern gadgets.

By late 1935, these little just-for-camping vehicles were averaging over seventeen feet in length. And they needed every foot, because here are a few of the amenities they contained:

- kerosene, coal, or wood-burning heaters
- two- to four-burner gasoline cookstoves, with ovens
- dual lighting systems, running off either the 6-volt car battery or a 110-volt outside supply
- twenty-five- to fifty-pound iceboxes
- tiled bathrooms, with chemical toilets and lavatories
- twenty-gallon water tanks, with marine-style hand pumps beside each sink or lavatory
- enameled or galvanized steel sinks
- fold-away writing desks
- built-in radios, their antenna wires buried in the roof
- full-sized beds with innerspring mattresses
- screened, crank-operated roof ventilators
- electric exhaust fans over the cookstove
- felt, rock wool, or foil insulation in walls and ceilings
- Venetian blinds and curtains at every window
- dinettes and full-sized sofas
- full-length closets with mirrored doors

All this in a box barely six feet wide, a little over six feet high, and less than fourteen honest feet in length—for manufacturers had already adopted the dubious practice of including the hitch in their length measurements, and hitches averaged between two and three feet. So a seventeen-foot model would have a body length of, say, fourteen and a half feet, and an inside (useable space) measurement of fourteen feet or less, depending on how curvy and streamlined the ends of the trailer were.

By 1935 some of these stubby little wonders had gotten so elaborate and so overweight they needed third wheels—dollies—under the hitch to take some of the load off the towcar. It was obvious that in its gadgetry (manufacturers preferred the term "appointments") the lowly camp trailer was moving steadily closer to the chromeplated luxury of Glenn Curtiss's Land Yachts.

Meanwhile, what about the plywood shell that enclosed all these appointments? Trailer design, even more than other design fields in the early thirties, ran wild. With so little communication between them, each builder was free to follow his own genius—or lack thereof. Models

"There was hardly an order that we received in those days that didn't have some special request. Could this be built in, or that? We built in so many gadgets. . . ."
—Airstream founder Wally Byam, in *Trailer Travel Here and Abroad*

or patterns to imitate, beyond the obvious ones of chicken shack and outhouse, were scarce. Imaginations soared. Out in Los Angeles a man named R. T. Baumberger, doing business as the Columbia Trailer Company, was building trailers shaped like Pullman cars and painting them like gypsy wagons and selling them like hotcakes. He called them "Travel-Omes." It was this same Baumberger, incidentally, who starting in 1933 organized the very first caravan tours among American trailerites—an idea Wally Byam of Airstream reinvented after World War II and promoted into an international event.

Even the sane and conservative Arthur Sherman had a brief fling with aesthetics. His business was hardly off the ground before he stripped the boxy body off his basic cart and replaced it with a tall, hoop-roofed structure that was clearly an attempt to create, out of thin and flexible masonite, a true 'covered wagon' look. What he achieved instead was an almost perfect replica of the Wyoming sheepherder's wagon—not exactly a status symbol west of Omaha.

Did true covered wagons have side windows? They did not—and neither did Mr. Sherman's replica. Despite the added headroom (you could almost stand up inside this hooproofed model, and without lowering the kitchen floor) sales immediately dropped off. Poor ventilation made the little coaches hot and claustrophobic inside. Your true covered wagon, it seems, was somewhat bigger than six by nine. And draftier, too—not built half so well. While other trailer makers were busy copying cabooses and yachts and stage coaches and even submarines, Arthur Sherman went straight back to the box. Not the boxy box, of course—that was passé. What Sherman adopted was the new box, the thirties box—the streamlined box.

"Streamline" was the buzzword of the early thirties—an outgrowth of the widespread interest in aviation that Lindbergh had awakened with his New York-to-Paris flight in '27. Chrysler demonstrated the streamline principle all too vividly with the 1934 'Airflow,' a radical, droop-snooted beast that people who had grown up with square cars—meaning everybody—hated on sight. New streamlined trains and ships and busses were rushed into service, amid the popping of flashbulbs and champagne corks and as much hoopla as the railroad and steamship and bus lines could muster.

"Whatever you're selling, streamline it! Don't throw them old molds away—just round off the corners some. It's gotta be streamlined to sell!"

Aircraft engineers, many of whom hadn't worked since 1930, found themselves suddenly in demand to design almost everything: ashtrays and coffee urns and table lamps and skyscrapers and a thousand other geegaws that, barring major catastrophe, seemed unlikely to fly. Streamline was in; horse and buggy was out. And trailermen were no different from anyone else: they wanted to be in.

Old Glenn Curtiss, had he lived, would have seen his rounded bread-loaf roof, which he first used on the Motor Bungalow of 1917, slapped onto hundreds of otherwise boxy and unsophisticated house trailer designs—to make them more streamlined. One of the most successful trailermen of the prewar decade, a thin, nervous, blond-haired chap named Norman Christian Wolfe, took his company name—Silver Dome—from this domelike roof shape, which he covered with tent fabric and waterproofed with aluminized paint, in what became the standard practice of the day.

Other builders tried V-shaped prows on their little boxes, only to find that a sharp snout, besides wasting inside space, can actually generate more turbulence and drag at highway speeds than a blunt one. "Boattails" enjoyed a brief vogue in trailers, as they had in automobiles. So did parrot beaks and bullet noses and ridiculous back ends that tapered off like banana slugs.

Along toward the middle of the decade, however, order began to emerge from this chaos of shape and misshape. It's one thing to warp plywood and masonite into flamboyant twists and curves for your family's own personal trailer, but builders turning out their second—or their second hundredth—model found themselves thinking of ways to simplify the design, ways to work more flat sections into their curvaceous little beauties. Without losing that streamlined look, of course.

What emerged were two distinct schools of thought, based on roof shape. One school settled upon a kind of shoebox beneath the Curtiss dome or bread-loaf roof, rounded on every side. Most of the major builders of the decade—Covered Wagon, Vagabond, Schult, Indian, Kozy Coach, Palace, and of course Silver Dome—belonged to this school. They preferred the phrase "coach style" rather than "bread-loaf" to describe their roofs, fancying that they were imitating the shape of

"The trailer industry is a young one and you are not limited to many standardized designs, shapes, colors or sizes."
—*Popular Mechanics,*
December 1936

York Cruiser display at the Eastern States Fair, 1936. The York was a typical caravan or "ham can" trailer, with flat walls and square corners. Coach or "bread-loaf" styles, like the Silver Dome hiding behind the sign, were more popular.

a railway coach roof. Nevertheless, what their creations resembled more than anything else was a loaf of homemade bread wrapped in aluminum foil, with windows and wheels and a funny little smokestack.

The second school of design originated in England. At least three companies—Split-Coach in Pennsylvania, Trotwood in Ohio, and Airstream out in Los Angeles—had obviously been peeking at a British trailering magazine called *The Caravan*—or maybe just the English trailer ads in *Punch*—for early in the decade they started producing slavish imitations of the typical English "caravan" style.

Trotwood introduced the first of these in 1932, and it became immediately popular. They called it the "Ranger." It was a short, flatsided, flat-roofed vehicle with rounded front and back that had, in profile, something of the shape of a ham can stood on edge. This ham can shape immediately became a classic, the second of the two body styles that was to dominate the American house trailer industry until the coming of the mobile homes in the 1950s. Even today, most camping trailers, with the exception of the Airstream and its imitators, still use a kind of squared-off version of the 1930s hamcan, or caravan, style.

The Split-Coach Corporation, a small company in York, Pennsylvania, started building a line of camp trailers in the late twenties, a year or two before Arthur Sherman. When the February 1931 *Scientific American* gave Sherman's six by nine Covered Wagon its one and only national writeup, our bacteriologist's trailer had to share the spotlight with what was obviously a vastly more sophisticated Split-Coach model—a wheeled box with twice as many windows, three more feet of length, and an ability to split open and accordion out, forming a room twelve feet square and over seven feet high. Twelve by twelve! By the standards of the day, the Split-Coach was a giant among camp trailers, a veritable rolling ballroom.

Was the Split-Coach expensive? It was. But just look inside: four big Pullman-style berths, a wash basin and full kitchenette, two large folding tables, cupboards and drawers and storage bins everywhere. Down the middle of the ceiling ran a Pullman-style night curtain that divided the room in half so two couples could share quarters in relative privacy. The Split-Coach: clearly years ahead of the father of the American trailer industry. Wasn't the modest medicine man from Detroit embarrassed?

Not a bit.

"Too complex," muttered Sherman. Besides, the accordion mechanism depended on canvas, and Arthur George Sherman had gotten his fill of wet canvas, back in the Michigan woods in the summer of '28. He went right on making his rigid, non-folding, non-telescoping, uncomplicated little masonite boxes. With streamlined corners, and without hoop roofs.

And history, as it turned out, was on Arthur Sherman's side. By 1935, Split-Coach had abandoned their split coaches and joined the Sherman camp—the hard-shell camp. But bread-loaves were not for them. Their two "York Cruisers," Junior and Senior, were English caravans to the core, with flat sides, flattish roofs and bulging ends: plywood ham cans, with a flair. Both were just a little more curvy and quaint, a little more baroque than your plain-jane Trotwood Ranger. The Junior, for example, had clip-on latticework over the door glass to

"Lacking the crudeness of a tent . . . it has on the contrary all the excellence of a fine living room. It is the place where exacting people who refuse to go motor camping may be happy and comfortable."
—Split-Coach ad in *MoToR Magazine*, January 1930

"Don't buy a trailer with a canvas roof."
—Morley Cooper, *The Trailer Book* (1950)

give it the true fake English cottage look, while the Senior model
sported a clerestory or lantern-style roof, the section down the middle
being raised a few inches, like a Mohawk haircut, for extra headroom
in the main aisle. Clerestory roofs were a specialty of British caravan
makers. They were a distinctive styling touch, reminiscent of the roofs
on nineteenth-century railroad cars; they permitted additional windows
and vents down either side, which kept the trailers cooler inside. But
they proved to be a bit too pricey to build, as even the English finally
had to concede, and they pretty well ran their course before Hitler's
war.

Meanwhile, out in Los Angeles, an aggressive young printer named
Wallace Byam, who started trailer building in the late twenties with a
tent platform on a Model T axle, had just evolved a sleek, impractical,
thirteen-foot canvas and masonite teardrop he called the "Torpedo,"
when, about 1933, he too discovered the English caravan. Here at last
was a design round enough to pass for modern, yet with interior space
for more than one person at a time. This caravan shape looked like a
winner—and it was. In the spring of 1935 Wally Byam ceased to be
Byam Press, selling plans and parts and printed instructions to do-it-
yourself trailer tinkerers. He became instead the Airstream Trailer Company, a full-time manufacturer of flat-sided, flatroofed English caravan
look-alikes.

These Airstream caravans—Tom Mix took delivery on an early
one—were larger and more handsome than the Trotwood Ranger, almost as curvy and quaint as the Split-Coach models. They were full of
unexpected humps and bulges that made them interesting to look at
but hell to build. Byam had the heart of a showman; he couldn't resist
circusy paint jobs: bright, contrasting color bands that curved and
swooped around the windows, down the sides, up and over the roof.
People who liked this Gypsy Moderne look loved it. People who didn't
had eighty-four other trailer builders in the Los Angeles basin to choose
from—for Wally Byam was never the man to brook criticism.

Though Byam couldn't have known it at the time, these gaudy little
masonite boxes were only a stopgap for Airstream, a way of keeping
up the cashflow until better things came along. Byam had not yet met
the aeronautical wizard William Hawley Bowlus. He had not yet seen
the aluminum jellybean that Bowlus was riveting together up in the

San Fernando Valley, the trailer design destined to make Wally Byam wealthy, destined to make trailering—in this nation of two billion wheels, this country that has been called an experiment in transportation—almost respectable.

So where was all this early thirties evolution of shape and size and gadgetry headed? It was headed in a direction that did not please Arthur George Sherman, bacteriologist; a direction that made Wally Byam positively livid. It was headed away from the camp trailer and toward the house trailer. Away from sport, recreation, and pastime—toward an entirely new way of life.

> The typical trailer is a mobile one-room, light- housekeeping apartment, with bathroom included, although there are large models which have more accommodations (*The New York Times,* September 15, 1935).

> Structurally, the trailer is like a modern home, insulated against summer's heat and winter's cold, and having practically every convenience which makes for good and comfortable living (*Popular Science,* July 1935).

> It must be borne in mind, too, that although the traveling home can travel, it can also settle down, providing all the economies of the trailer car together with the advantages of a fixed residence (*The American Mercury,* September 1935).

House trailers. All those little camp trailers the manufacturers were turning out were starting to be mistaken for *house* trailers. And not just by America's journalists—that would be bad enough—but by the folk who owned them.

> A million people, in the estimate of the American Automobile Association, are living in them for part or all of the year. Most of the year-round crowd follow the birds south in Autumn, north in Spring, but many stay planted on vacant lots and ramble not at all. Omaha, for one city, reports 300 families living there in trailers throughout the year (*The New York Times,* November 1, 1936).

Living in them for part or all of the year. This was the real news story, when the media finally discovered the house trailer, in mid-1935. But the reporters were deliberately distracted from this story by the manufacturers. Their attention was discreetly drawn away from trailer

"It is . . . inevitable that people should think of trailers as permanent dwellings."
—American Municipal Association, report #114, February 1937

customers, the folk standing in line to buy these miniature wheeled houses. Their attention was focused instead upon the trailers themselves—those gaudy little boxes that whispered of sea breezes and warm sand, of freedom with order, of adventure with security—the trailers themselves, and the thriving companies that were building them to backorder lists some six or eight months long. With a little help from the manufacturers, the reporters managed to overlook the people story in favor of the business story. And no wonder—good news business stories were rare enough in America in the year 1935.

"The 400-odd manufacturers would like to hear as little as possible about the trailer as a permanent address."
—*Literary Digest*, November 14, 1936

So the media mobbed the manufacturers, hung on their every word, made overnight heroes of them. A flood of newspaper and magazine stories painted the trailermen as the last torch-bearers of capitalism and free enterprise and Yankee ingenuity, the heroic pioneers of a brave new industry that was just about to rescue the nation's foundering economy and break the back of the six-year-old depression—just about to put America on its feet again.

Such predictions made good copy—and they might even turn out to be true. After all, hadn't Roger Babson himself said so?

4 Escape Taxes and Rent

If she slight me when I woo,
I can scorn and let her go.
  For if she be not for me,
  What care I for whom she be?
    —George Wither (1588–1677)

Many people still living remember the name Roger Ward Babson. The good Mr. Babson—he died in 1967, at the venerable age of 92—was once dean of American financial advisors. Throughout the twenties his investment advice appeared in syndicated newspaper columns from Maine to California. Thousands subscribed to *Babson's Reports,* a weekly compendium of moral platitudes and market analysis that emanated from his headquarters in Wellesley, Massachusetts. When Babson chanced to predict, with uncanny accuracy, the market crash of 1929, he was immediately elevated to a kind of secular sainthood, approaching that of Thomas Edison, that of Henry Ford himself. By the early thirties Roger Ward Babson could say no wrong; he had become the Walter Cronkite of America's depression years.

Yet few of those people who remember Babson seem willing recall, without prompting, his second most famous prediction, mumbled quietly in 1935 and repeated more loudly in the premier issue of *Trailer Travel* magazine the following spring. "Within two decades," Babson ventured, "one out of every two Americans will be living in a trailer." What? Half the country? Living in house trailers? Had the good grey prophet of Wall Street lost his mind?

"The trailer generated its own wild enthusiasts."
—*Harpers,* April 1938

He had not. He had lost his heart.

Roger Babson turned out to be dead wrong, of course, just one more

A brief tour of the parks in Florida and southern California in 1935 convinced respected economist Roger Babson that half of America would one day live on wheels.

victim of a new contagion that would soon come to be known as "trailer fever." The economist and his wife had spent a few idyllic weeks touring south Florida in a borrowed Curtiss Land Yacht, a ten-thousand-dollar custom-built coach with two bathrooms and complete servants' quarters—thirty-five feet of airconditioned spaceship, upholstered inside and out with leather and chrome and money. During part of the icy winter of 1934–35, the Babsons cruised from one palm-lined Florida estate to another in the Land Yacht's chauffeured luxury, parking beside six-car garages and taking most of their meals out. To Roger Babson, who owned a mansion in Massachusetts and a whole town—Babson Park—in central Florida, this was the simple life, the gypsy life, the healthful and invigorating life of the great outdoors. Everyone, he felt, should try it.

When Babson discovered by a little informal research that thousands were already trying it, that the three-hundred-odd trailer camps of the Sunshine State were full to overflowing every winter with Yankees and locals alike, that the infant trailer industry in 1935 appeared to be almost the only growth industry in the whole stagnant nation—he felt certain that he had glimpsed the future.

Within twenty years half of America will be living on wheels.

His words set the country on its ear, sent journalists and photographers from *Life, Time, The Saturday Evening Post, Harper's, The Christian Science Monitor*—virtually every major magazine and newspaper in the United States—scrambling wildly about trying to answer the questions everyone was suddenly asking: What are these house trailers, anyway? Who makes them? Who's buying them? And then the kicker: Are people really selling their homes and moving into them to live?

The story the reporters uncovered surprised even Babson himself. Out of the depths of the Great Depression a brand-new industry had arisen. Every crossroads town in the country, it seemed, had its little side street trailer factory, and every one of these trailer factories, the reporters found, had two things in common: they couldn't build trailers fast enough, and they couldn't build trailers big enough.

If you could corner him for ten minutes, each trailer builder would tell you pretty much the same story: he'd begun with simple vacation models, little masonite tents on wheels. But suddenly his customers were wanting—demanding—far more than just a bed and a stove and a solid roof over their heads. Suddenly they wanted porcelain sinks and huge closets and inlaid linoleum. They wanted toilets and lavatories and tiled shower stalls, full-length mirrors and whatnot shelves, space heaters and built-in radios. In short, they wanted everything you'd find in a modern efficiency apartment—all wrapped in a package small enough to tow behind their six-cylinder coupe. And they wanted it now.

Who are these customers, the journalists asked? Here the manufacturers shrugged, and their eyes cut to one side. They hadn't the faintest idea; movie stars and rich people and retired bankers, they guessed—

"[Babson] estimated that already 300,000 to 500,000 Americans were living on wheels. After interviewing hundreds of rolling-home owners, he ascribed this amazing tendency to a revolt against . . . misgovernment, high taxes, and economic insecurity."
—*Saturday Evening Post,* May 23, 1936

"Beyond question the trailer is the most excitingly portentous gadget at hand today."
—*Fortune,* March 1937

all kinds of people, probably. With production running six months behind demand, nobody really had time—or reason—to care. "Just make 'em a little bigger, a little fancier than last year's model, and people will stand in line for 'em. There's some kind of crazy fad going on out there. Damn near anything with two wheels and a porcelain sink will sell. . . ."

This house trailer, it seemed, was the coming gadget. It was, according to Roger Babson and the raucous flock of philosopher-journalists who followed up on his story, just about to rescue the nation's foundering economy, shake the country out of its of its six-year lethargy, become the new key to prosperity. *Vide*: In all of America, the trailer industry alone couldn't hire enough help, couldn't fill even half its orders. Three hundred thousand customers were waiting impatiently for their Covered Wagons, Airfloats, Kozy-Coaches, Schults, Trotwoods, Vagabonds, Travelezes, Aladdins, Palaces, Generals, Nomads, Hayeses, Bowluses, Millers, Stage Coaches, Almas, Benders, Roycrafts, Airstreams, Masterbilts, Prairie Schooners, Quakers, Pioneers, Travelos, Elcars, Halscos, Harrises, Stream-lites—or any one of hundreds of other brands that sprang suddenly from cabinet shops and back-yard garages of Michigan, Ohio, southern California, Pennsylvania, Wisconsin, and Illinois. All across the nation the headlines and editorials agreed: the Mobile Age was here.

America's brief romance with the house trailer had begun.

Mechanically, the trailer is as sound as the car that pulls it. Structurally, the trailer is like a modern home, insulated against summer's heat and winter's cold, and having practically every convenience which makes for good and comfortable living (*Popular Mechanics,* July 1935).

The automobile trailer has become a national institution. There are now two hundred and fifty thousand of them on the highways (*American Mercury,* September 1935).

The modern trailer is no longer an ugly wooden box. Anywhere from 14 to 22 feet long, it is a streamlined lozenge of light metal [sic] with curtained windows, chromium fittings, a simple swivel joint at the bow where it couples with the automobile. Inside, it is as compactly luxurious as the cabin of a small cruiser (*Time,* June 15, 1936).

Five years ago it was just a convenience for motor tourists, an overnight shelter, usually homemade, a mobile bedroom dragged along behind the car. Today it is a fairly complete home, factory-built, and it is the only home of thousands of Americans who have gone gypsy (*The New York Times Magazine,* November 1, 1936).

The automobile trailer is the old, restless pioneer blood in the American veins, and it is the American passion for material comforts (*The New York Times,* November 16, 1936).

Go anywhere, stop anywhere, escape taxes and rent—this is irresistible. Nothing but death has ever before offered so much in a single package (*Automotive Industries,* December 1936).

It is a new way of life—a new way of life which will eventually change our architecture, our morals, our laws, our industrial system, and our system of taxation (*Harpers,* May 1937).

The country was dazzled, charmed by these little homes on wheels. The brave new world they promised fired the American imagination, touched something deep and restless within the nation's spirit. Here was all the romance of the private yacht, all the conveniences of the modern apartment, fitted into a neat little streamlined box. Think of it: a house without a lot! What a marvelous new concept! By simply severing the age-old tie between shelter and real estate, you create affordable housing for the masses. Why hadn't anyone thought of this before?

"And they say there's a feller up in Chicago selling 'em on time, no money down—lets you park free on his own land 'til the loan's paid off. You know, old Babson just might be right—we just might be on the verge of some kind of social revolution here!"

Some kind of social revolution. . . .

Slowly the implications of the trailer as home began to sink in. A million cute little portable bungalows to solve America's housing shortage had seemed, at first glance, a quaint idea. But a million portable homes meant three million, four million portable *people*—people in need, no matter where they went, of fresh water and sewage disposal and police and fire protection, of schools and libraries and health care and streets. Three million, four million wanderers—nomads—gypsies.

At this point the reporters went scurrying out to the camps to find out exactly who these people were. And immediately they saw that

Manufacturers tried to counter the trailer's gypsy image by pretending that movie stars and industrialists were their biggest customers. But most trailerites like these in Dennisport, Massachusetts (1936) were just average, working-class Americans.

these trailer folk weren't as well-to-do as the manufacturers had seemed to imply. They weren't all retired bankers, and they certainly weren't movie stars. They were old folk and young folk, working folk and retired, blue-collar folk and white-collar folk, but mostly blue—pretty much the same people who had been sitting around campfires a decade earlier singing "your friends are my friends and my friends are your friends." A few of these trailerites were rich, a few were poor—but on the whole they were just . . . folk. Some of the men in the camps seemed to think nothing of going abroad in their undershirts, even on Sunday.

Mornings, the women all trooped to the bathrooms in their housecoats and curlers, waving toothbrushes at one another unself-consciously. On washday, they hung their laundry out.

They hung their laundry out! Not only did these trailer people do their own wash, they hung it out to dry, right before God and everyone! Would movie stars do that? Would the wealthy do that? Slowly the editorial voice began to lose its tone of infatuation:

> A rolling home gathers no moss; but how long can the 1,000,000 persons riding around in automobile trailers escape the issue of mounting taxes, rising registration fees, and soaring insurance costs? (*The Christian Science Monitor,* October 7, 1936).

> We are rapidly becoming a nation on wheels. Today hundreds of thousands of families have packed their possessions into traveling houses, said goodbye to their friends, and taken to the open roads . . . [soon] more families will take to the road, making an important proportion of our people into wandering gypsies (editorial, *The New York Times,* December 20, 1936).

> Health hazards may pile up in trailers—plumbingless, water supply from anywhere, food preparation haphazard, refrigeration doubtful or lacking. Social workers are haunted by visions of trailer slums, when the once-comfortable portable home has become a hand-me-down (*Survey Graphic,* January 1937).

> TRAILERS BRING FAMILIES AND PROBLEMS (headline, *Nation's Business,* February 7, 1937).

> Like Chinese ports and rivers, crowded with houseboats, we have a floating population. At least a million persons now lead a gypsy life that knows no care for the morrow, with the prospect that a year hence there will be two million. . . . The man who drags his house after him has about as much sense of fixity as a tramp (editorial, *The New York Times,* February 9, 1937).

> An epidemic couldn't get off to a more blazing start than in some of these crowded rookeries ("200,000 Trailers," *Fortune,* March 1937).

> In fact, the gasoline gypsy pays less for social services than any other citizen in these taxridden United States (editorial, *The New York Times,* May 4, 1937).

The trailer abolishes the home and with it State lines and State citizenship (editorial, *The New York Times,* May 15, 1937).

CALLS AUTO TRAILER A MENACE TO HEALTH (headline, *The New York Times,* May 26, 1937).

Communicable diseases—typhoid fever, smallpox, influenza and all the rest—are spread fastest by travel. With thousands of persons traveling constantly, many of whom have never traveled before, the spread of disease may be greatly accelerated (*Science News Letter,* July 3, 1937).

A highly mobile population of problematical size may be created, in which the traditional home, which has its roots in a single locality and is controlled by neighborhood mores, may be abandoned (*Report of the National Resources Committee,* July 1937).

Many of the so-called "nomads" have created a new problem by settling down in one spot; in other words, taking up permanent residence in a motorless trailer (*The New York Times,* September 19, 1937).

SMALLPOX—TYPHOID—TRAILER CAMPS (headline, *American City,* November 1937).

Who should bear the responsibility for the wandering hosts, living briefly here and there as squatters, rootless as air plants, paying no taxes, creating a new kind of motor slums? (*Fortune,* March 1937).

"Before resorting to trailers, some of the Navy men were paying out as much as 60 per cent of their wages for rent."
—*Trailer Topics,* July 1937

Who were these rebels, these gasoline gypsies "rootless as air plants," who were suddenly threatening the American home, the tax structure, the Constitution, community morals, states' rights, property values, public health, our cities, the future of our children? Where did they all come from? Who was giving them their marching orders? Were they reds, pinkos, bolshies in disguise? Was this the beginning of the revolution—the great, angry, middle-class uprising that people had been predicting ever since the market collapsed in '29?

5 Who Goes There?

Probably the principal attraction of the trailer was its promise of escape from long-accepted social practices.

—Harpers,
April 1938

Pitchmen, vaudeville troupes, circus people are going in for trailers.

—Fortune,
March 1937

My father, who liked to call himself an Ohio farm boy, was a short, dark, powerful man with a catlike independence of spirit and a terrier's stubbornness and tenacity. After his mother died in 1937, when he was 33, I doubt that he did more than half a dozen things that he really didn't want to do, all the rest of his life—and he lived to be 72.

He met and married my mother, a 34-year-old Cincinnati newspaper woman, in 1939—his third marriage, her first. The following spring they bought an eighteen-foot Schult Master and joined those wandering hosts who were out to destroy America, those wild-eyed and rebellious trailerites. Before their marriage, neither had lived outside the state of Ohio for more than a few weeks; after their marriage they never lived within that state for more than five months running.

Family stories of their early years together play, in my mind's theater at least, like scenes from *The Taming of the Shrew*. Example: An A&P supermarket in New Orleans, circa 1941. Big sale on toilet paper. My father, in his impeccably starched and ironed bricklayer's khaki, tosses not one, not two, but six rolls into the shopping cart, to take home to the little Schult's three-by-three-foot chemical-toilet bathroom. My mother—tall, handsome, aloof, an opera-goer and supervisor, before

> "[Mr. and Mrs. Burns] started out in the fall of 1934 to come south for the winter, and they liked the trailer so fine that they'd been in the thing ever since."
> —*The Saturday Evening Post*, May 23, 1936

her marriage, of a twenty-eight-woman office—says half-innocently (but only half): "David, what in heaven's name are you going to do with all that tissue?" And David, nostrils flaring, voice raised for the benefit of people still out in the parking lot, replies: "Emily, I intend to wipe my A-double-Que with it!" End of scene.

I have come to see these two strong-willed and autonomous individuals as archetypical trailerites—near-perfect examples of the type of person who was drawn to trailer life in the pioneering period. Neither of them was entirely comfortable in the 1930s middle-class mold. My mother, a tall, slender, dark-eyed career woman who took university night courses and stayed single into her mid-thirties; my dad, twice divorced, an arrogantly successful contractor in '29, broke by '35 and living on a houseboat tied up at the Cincinnati piers.

For their honeymoon, my father threw his canvas satchel of bricklaying tools into the trunk of their LaSalle coupe—it was muggy August in the Ohio Valley—and they motored off to cool Quebec, where he worked a few weeks in Trois-Rivières, the only man on the job who spoke no French. From there they wandered down to Niagara Falls and the New York World's Fair, and finally south through Atlanta and Mobile and New Orleans to the Texas coast as winter came on.

The southern sun delighted them both; why fight those bleak midwestern winters if you don't have to? And of course they didn't—a good bricklayer could find work anywhere. But they hated living in strange hotels and rooming houses (in a nicer than average hotel in New Orleans they were advised to set their luggage on newspapers and surround it with roach poison). So when spring came, they packed the LaSalle and followed the geese northward to the little Indiana town of Elkhart, where a man named Wilbur Schult was manufacturing masonite bungalows on wheels.

It's one of the ironies of history that construction workers—masons and carpenters and plumbers and painters and all the rest of the seventeen building trades—were among the house trailer's earliest and most loyal adherents. For these skilled artisans were—according to the social prophets of the mid-thirties—just about to be put out of work by the coming "trailer revolution," when half of America's houses would no longer be built on site, but would roll off factory assembly lines just like any other consumer good. Former SAE president William Bushnell

"The present trailer population is made up chiefly of naturally inclined nomads, itinerant laboring people, retired couples [and] families too poor to rent or buy."
—*Trailer Topics*, Summer 1938 issue

"[Trailers offer] a delightful combination of security and vagabondism."
—*Trailer Topics*, August 1939

Stout, designer of the Ford Trimotor airplane, had said as much, and the radical young architect who invented the geodesic dome, a man with the unlikely name of Buckminster Fuller, agreed.

Buckminster Fuller, for all his trailer enthusiasm, was not my father's idea of an architect; Frank Lloyd Wright was. Wright was the underground hero at Ohio State when my father studied architecture there during the twenties; and besides, Wright designed in brick and stone, not ticky-tacky. "That's a beautiful place," Emily would say of some brick house we passed (she had learned never to admire frame houses in the presence of my dad). "Veneer!" David would snort in contempt, "Nothing but a termite trap!" He could tell brick veneering from a block away. No structure with wood in it pleased this feisty, fastidious little master mason. And yet he and my mother chose to live, for part if not all of every year between 1940 and 1955, in a flimsy plywood cabin on wheels.

Cranks, both of them. Eccentrics—and archetypical trailerites.

The few studies done on prewar trailer dwellers bear this out. Most of these first-generation gypsies were married, middle-income midwesterners, city dwellers before they bought their first rig, above average in education, with (statistically) half a child to accompany them. This describes my parents, almost to a T. The median age of the thirties trailerite was 45, but this figure, as well as the low childcount, simply reflects the high percentage of retirees among those drawn to this curious new life.

Here, for the record, are some of the kinds of people that writers reported meeting in the thirties parks: sign painters, retired Army personnel, cannery workers, former bank presidents, barbers, carpenters, vacationing schoolteachers, artists, industrial workers, WPA employees, army and navy pilots, advance men for carnivals, students, writers, geologists, sculptors, prospectors, ministers, fortunetellers, musicians, newspaper editors, a performer with a trained donkey, a man and wife toy-making team, salesmen beyond number, pipeliners, baseball players, surveyors, an entire circus in a forty-trailer caravan, fishermen, lecturers, construction workers and oilfield workers by the dozen.

If a single word had to be chosen to describe these trailer pioneers, that word would be "unconventional." Or so it seems from the perspective of a half century. But that's not how people saw them at the

"We're landlubbers out here in the Midwest—we can't have sea-going yachts; so we'll have land-going yachts."
—Letter to the Editor, *Trailer Travel*, January–February 1936

time. At the time, the growing trailer movement appeared to be nothing short of revolutionary—a threat to the American way of life that seemed even more immediate, more tangible, than the menace of Russian bolshevism.

In this second half—our half—of the twentieth century, *revolt* has once more become the prerogative of youth, just as it was in the nineteenth century, just as the founders of the Romantic movement intended it to be. The scenario of revolt goes something like this: Parents and grandparents man the barricades of conventional wisdom. Young people, powerless and angry, rise up to storm and destroy and overrun those barricades. When the smoke clears and the adrenaline ebbs, sure enough, the barricades are down, and the young find themselves on the other side—their parents' side—with barely time to turn around and rebuild the defenses before the coming of the next onslaught, led by their own angry children, flying a slightly different flag and following close on their heels. And so it goes.

But history hasn't always been at the mercy of impetuous youth. The revolutionaries of the 1930s, for example, weren't confined to any single age or social group. The angry young men of America's Great Depression were, as often as not, in their fifties or sixties—and female.

The collapse of the Western world's economic system during the early thirties came as a profound shock to people of all ages. Suddenly the core values they had taken for granted since birth—hard work, honesty, loyalty, thrift—wouldn't buy them so much as a cup of coffee. How can you work hard when there are no jobs? What does it mean to be honest when you have so little power, so little opportunity to be otherwise? And as for thrift, the idea of socking away a portion of each dollar you earn, as Ben Franklin advised—well, you can't very well save what you never had.

The Great Depression reduced millions of Americans of every age and class to the powerless and angry condition of adolescence. Some fell into despair, even suicide. Some joined the Communist party and attacked the barricades directly. Some drifted west to begin life anew; some simply drifted. Others—the vast majority—clung to their oars, paddled harder, and admonished one another through clenched teeth not to rock the boat.

But a few people saw opportunity amid all this chaos—opportunity

Retirees were quick to adopt this new way of life, even though it violated so many of the social norms of the day.

to rebuild their world, their values, along more personal and perhaps less vulnerable lines. Among these rebuilders were the pioneer trailerites of the thirties, over a million strong. Idealists and iconoclasts, thoughtful and deliberate drop-outs. People who chose not to wait for big government or big business to save them, who chose to take their economic destiny back into their own hands. People who elected to slip the middle-class noose and form for themselves a wholly new subculture—a life just a little freer, a little more autonomous and less anxiety-ridden, a little closer to their hearts' desires.

In doing so, they made a lot of enemies, for they stretched, distorted, and ultimately broke many of the social norms and conventions of their time.

From today's perspective, the conventions that the pioneer trailerites violated may appear dim and insipid. The great taboos of the past are always faintly amusing. After all, we've outgrown them. Somewhere along the line, somebody broke them and lived; somebody broke them, and the heavens didn't fall. Only our current taboos, the yet unbroken ones, are deadly serious.

Here, then, are a few of the conventions, the unbroken taboos, that were deadly serious to most Americans in the thirties:

Family Ties. We tend to think that the old patterns of *grossfamilie*—three or more generations living under one roof—dissolved with the rise of industry and the decline of agriculture, somewhere back in the mists of the nineteenth century. It's sobering to recall that the first census to find more Americans living in cities than on the farm was the census of 1920—just nine years before Arthur Sherman began peddling his little two-wheeled vacation cabins to the citizens of Detroit. Until well after World War I, the United States was—both statistically and emotionally—a nation of farmers. People not actually born on the farm still tended to have rural backgrounds, with parents and grandparents, aunts and uncles, still in the country. This was especially true in the midwest, where the bulk of America's trailer pioneers originated.

Formality. Newspapers and magazines covering the early trailer movement seldom failed to mention the casual dress of the trailerites, the "shirt-sleeve society" of the camps. Why? Because it was in such noticeable contrast to the accepted dress of the time. The dress code of the mid-thirties called for women in calf-length skirts, men in suit coats or sport coats, even—no, *especially*—at the posh resort hotels where Americans had traditionally vacationed. And, of course, the white-collar men simply did not go to work without coat and tie, just as their wives, with few exceptions, did not go to work at all.

Journalists and photographers of the thirties, people who prided

---

"We weren't the sort, we kept telling ourselves grimly, who went on relief or asked for help from the relatives."
—"You *Can* Take 'Em With You," a trailerite mother's story in *The Saturday Evening Post,* August 14, 1937

Laundry was an almost daily chore for the trailerite. Wardrobes were small, and there was little room for dirty clothes to accumulate. The better parks had fenced drying areas, but in most the wash was hung wherever there was room.

themselves on being at the jaunty, bohemian fringe of sartorial respectability, came rolling into those early trailer camps—and immediately felt overdressed. For here were women in pants—in shorts, even—and men in polo shirts (or, worse yet, undershirts) and trousers. A few of the older men still sported the bright red suspenders of the 1920s motor gypsy crowd, just to show that they were sure-enough tin canners. Why, these people, these trailerites, weren't dressed—they were undressed!

And they were shockingly open collared, too: except on Sunday mornings, hardly a necktie was to be seen.

No ties? What respectable thirties male beyond highschool age dared

"A park is no different than any other place except that it is friendlier. . . . Few of them are formal."
—*Trailer Topics,* May 1939

show himself in public without a necktie? When college kids got together to swallow goldfish (the record, set at M.I.T. in 1938, was forty-two), they donned their sport coats—and ties. When a young man named John Warde stopped New York traffic for eleven hours before leaping to his death from the seventeenth-floor of the Hotel Gotham, he finally shed his suit coat—it was a sultry day—but it never occurred to him to loosen his tie.

And then there was the matter of laundry. Laundry, my God, draped everywhere! On ropes and wires and awning guys. Over the backs of lawn chairs. On hedges. In the lower branches of trees. These first trailer camps, grown so lately out of the tent camps of the motor gypsy crowd, were studies in sociology, not aesthetics. This practice of hanging the wash just anywhere was quickly curbed in the "better" camps, and fenced drying areas began appearing next to the laundry rooms. But photographers, throughout the house trailer's entire twenty-five-year history, never tired of setting up their overview shots of the parks with flying laundry in the foreground. They seemed to feel that only snapping sheets and dancing underwear captured the true spirit of trailerite informality.

Material Possessions. A house trailer had no basement, no attic, no spare bedroom, no shed. So the trailerite had to forgo much of the thing gathering that had already become the norm in America. To make the transition from house to trailer, every unnecessary item, every stick of furniture, every family heirloom, had to be sold, or passed on prematurely, or put in storage. Like emigrants from Europe, like covered wagon pioneers, trailer dwellers were forced to break most of their material ties to the past. Everything—every *thing*—a trailer family possessed had to fit into one of the vehicle's miniature cupboards, or under the bed, or into the trunk of the car.

"It is difficult for most of us to conceive of such living. We are too accustomed to space, to many rooms, to large and numerous articles of furniture."
—Freeman Marsh, *Trailers,* 1937

Even pets had to be portable. For years the fourth member of my own family was a cocker spaniel named Floppy. Although Floppy was never permitted inside the trailer—cockers *smell* much bigger than they are—his doghouse had to be vacuumed out and loaded into the living room, and Floppy himself into the car's back seat, every time we moved. Small wonder that canaries were the most common trailer pet, and quickly became a symbol of trailer life. (A 1930s camp in Berwyn,

Maryland, just north of Washington, D.C., was called The Modern Canary Trailer Park.)

Because of these space and weight considerations, trailerites were among the first twentieth-century Americans to keep their family ties but break the chain (some would say *chains*) of ownership: they deliberately stepped out of the world wide, centuries-old cycle of inherited property.

Privacy. By the beginning of the thirties, the front porch society of the turn of the century was already giving way to the impersonality of the electronic age. Next-door neighbors who, on mild evenings, might have talked and read and knitted and smoked together till dark were more and more to be found in their own parlors, listening to Amos 'n Andy or Major Bowes' Amateur Hour over the hum of an electric fan. The closed automobile, still a rarity in 1920, had by 1930 become the norm. Privacy, exclusivity, isolation—once the prerogatives of the very rich—had now moved within reach of the middle class.

But trailer society turned this whole ideal of privacy and exclusivity on its head—especially in the pioneer decade, when life on the parks was even more communal than it was to become after the war. Ralph Baker—one of the first journalists, incidentally, to bring the trailer movement to national attention—writing in Mencken's *American Mercury* in September of 1935 noted that in the camps he visited

> there appears to be developing a reversion to those amusements of earlier and simpler days. They get together and sing songs; a gifted one plays the guitar; a good story teller holds them enthralled; the men pitch horseshoes or play baseball. Some of the camps have community halls, and that is what they like best of all. Here they can congregate at night to dance, sing, or use the equipment.

Anyone familiar with the motor-camping movement of the previous decade might have told Baker where these anachronistic amusements came from: the gatherings of the tin can tourists, the motor gypsies. Still, such an open and sociable community of relative strangers was noticeably out of step with the accelerating trend toward privacy and impersonality in America during the thirties.

Regional Loyalty. "Once a Buckeye, always a Buckeye," my farm-bound uncle used to say. He couldn't understand why my father and mother would choose to live anywhere outside the glorious and God-favored state of Ohio. Every spring he turned over soil that had been in the family since 1802; to him my parents' actions seemed a deep disloyalty to the place of their birth—as if they had suddenly decided to emigrate to Czechoslovakia. He interpreted their leaving Ohio voluntarily as a slap in the face to those who stayed behind, an indictment of his own wisdom in choosing to remain.

On an even deeper level, I suspect, is the general human fear of rootlessness, the mistrust that wanderers, hitchikers, migrants and others who travel light have always caused among the sedentary—even if the wanderer happens to be a blood relation. In Europe, the sociologists tell us, those members of a gypsy clan who settle down on a piece of land, even as mere squatters, immediately begin to look down upon the rest of the clan who continue in the old nomadic traditions. It's the ancient fear the have-nots engender in the haves: "If you don't have what I have, then you must want it—hence you're a threat. If you don't have what I have and you don't want it, then you're a double threat, because obviously your values are skewed."

Hand in hand with loyalty to your state (township, village, family) went yet another vestige of feudalism: loyalty to your employer. As early as 1930, William Allen White called attention, in *The Saturday Evening Post,* to a new phenomenon in the American workforce—the migratory executive:

> Today the manager of a chain store may be in Oskaloosa, Iowa. Tomorrow he may be in Bellingham, Washington. Next year he may be in Daytona Beach, Florida; the year following, in New Haven, Connecticut. Always he is gypsy.

Although White's chain store manager caroms about the country, he still remains loyal to his home office, his company, his boss. But just five years later we find Roger Babson observing, of the trailerites he interviewed:

> Men whose professions are in demand throughout the nation are moving from city to city with their families, working in one town and leaving for another to improve their position whenever the opportunity affords itself.

"The stone that is rolling can gather no moss, For master and servant oft changing is loss."
—Thomas Tussers, 1573

No hint of company loyalty here. These mid-thirties trailerites leap about unpredictably, like jumping beans, like kids playing musical chairs—as employees do today.

To the people who stayed behind, the people who spent their entire lives in the same town, often in the same house, answering to the same boss for twenty, thirty, forty years, such job jumping and community hopping seemed the height of disloyalty, selfishness, and immaturity.

Retirement and Decline. For generations, old age and retirement had meant a contracting of activity, an acceptance of mental and physical decline. When you got too old to plow, you handed the reins to your kids and retired to the rocking chair to exude wisdom and tobacco smoke and await the grim reaper. That's what your parents had done, and their parents before them. That's simply what old people did.

But this new creation, the house trailer, offered the 1930s retiree another alternative: instead of settling back to die, he could set out to see the world—cheaply, and at pretty much his own speed. Pick up almost any book or magazine of the day and you could read about some trailerite doing just that—retiring to adventure. Padlocking the old homestead and heading for Florida, heading for the Rio Grande Valley, heading for Tucson or Phoenix or southern California.

Retire to adventure! By jingo, why not?

The kids, reins in hand, nose to the grindstone, saddled with the work of the world and busy raising children of their own, could think of any number of reasons why not: What if you get sick? What about your house and yard? Suppose you have car trouble? What will you do for friends? How will we know where to reach you?

But the old folks just hitched up their newfangled trailer and waved goodbye. They were no dummies; they could hear the whine between the lines: "You're too old to start living your life for fun! You're too old to become hedonists!"

The Work Ethic. Trailer life was, on the surface at least, a clear break with the tradition of making every minute count, of being "useful," of "improving your time"—in service to family, community, and your heirs. To simply loaf and invite your soul under some Florida palm tree was a flagrant waste of one's life and God-given talents, no more

"Too old to work, too
  young to die,
Two old lovers going
  bye-bye."
—Sign on back of travel
trailer, Florida, Missouri,
March 1988

The trailerite's striped-awning life made them appear to be on permanent vacation, regardless of whether they were retired or, like this San Diego construction foreman, working a six-day week.

socially acceptable in the mid-thirties than it had been in Walt Whitman's day.

Yet the trailerites, by the very nature of their striped-awning style of life, appeared to be on a sort of permanent vacation, regardless of whether they were retired or working six-day weeks. For they had stripped their lives of much of the regimentation and time-consuming chores that bound the homeowner: polishing furniture and painting gutters and trimming the yard and building fences and raking leaves and cleaning out the damned garage. The trailerite had begun, some twenty years ahead of the rest of working-class America, the conspicuous pursuit of leisure. It was not a popular move in the middle of the Great Depression.

"Here is a class who have achieved that much discussed condition— ample leisure time."
—*The American Mercury,* September 1935

The Sacred Home. Observers at the time—even those who were biased in favor of the trailer—worried about its effects on the American home. "Family disorganization and motley domestic assortments," grumbles an otherwise enthusiastic *Survey Graphic* editor in January, 1937, "loom as possibilities." Two months earlier, a writer for *The New York Times* had declared that "the arrival of the roadrunning residence is a serious matter. At the moment it looks to some eyes like a social upheaval, a revolution equal to Henry Ford's." This was an unconscious echo of critic Gilbert Seldes's apocalyptic warning that, because of the house trailer, America was "facing a movement of population beside which even the Crusades will seem like Sunday school picnics."

At the heart of such fears was the question of what was to happen to home and family if this gypsy life style continued to spread. Already the American family seemed to be shrinking and fragmenting, as the population continued its seemingly irreversible flow from country to city. Was the coming of the trailer destined to accelerate this trend?

Yes—according to a well-known sociology professor from Columbia University, Clyde E. Miller. Yes—but ultimately, no. Writing in *The New York Times* for Sunday, December 20, 1936, Miller asks, "What will the effects of this type of living be upon the family?" His answer:

> Sociologically, the entire concept of the family may change. Because space will be at a premium, the tendency toward smaller families will continue. Emphasis will be placed upon the minimum essentials of comfort; you cannot adorn your floating home with too many trinkets. The family will not feel its roots deeply planted in any community. . . . The children, especially, will be greatly affected. Soon there may be in this country thousands of children who will never know what it means to live in a regular house.

"However," Miller finally concludes, "I feel that America will not become a land of nomadic people. Basically, the American people are not of gypsy timber."

Which turned out to be so. The American people, or the vast majority of them, were not of gypsy timber. Only a million or so Americans were ever lured by the siren song of the house trailer during the true pioneer period, the prewar decade. Millions more looked wistfully at the little rolling homes speeding by and dreamed: If only I had the kind of job where I could move about. If only I didn't have kids in school. If only I were retired. If I wasn't stuck with this dadburn farm. If it was just me and Mabel. If only we were rich.

Journalists at the time made much of the fact that trailer living was not confined to any one economic class—that the same park might contain both a migrant crop picker's fifty-dollar home-built trailer and the sleek fifteen-thousand dollar custom land yacht of some wandering millionaire. And this did occasionally happen, for most of the early parks were wonderfully democratic: just the shared romance of living on wheels was enough to blur traditional class lines, at first.

But on the whole there were few class lines to blur in the trailer parks of the thirties, because the movement, or at least the individual parks, attracted mostly people of a similar class: people not so wealthy that they didn't cook their own food, nor yet so poor that they had no food to cook—working-class folk.

They were largely a self-selected sample of like-minded people: small town friendly and yet fiercely independent, for in the troubled days of the Great Depression it took a certain amount of grit to wave goodbye to Momma and launch the family down a strange highway, bound for an unknown town. The "Okies," the Dust Bowl migrants of Kansas and Texas and Oklahoma who took to the road in the thirties, did so because they had few other alternatives. The pioneer trailerites, for the most part, could have stayed home.

Strong-willed, unconventional folk.

From the very beginning, this radical new mode of living faced strong public prejudice, and people who took up trailering full-time needed thick hides. Even the most expensive factory-built rigs of the early thirties were almost indistinguishable, in the public eye, from the thousands of clumsy homebuilts that had preceded them. They looked, and traveled, and huddled in parks just like the crude packing crate trailers cobbled together in desperation by the mobile poor of the 1920s, the much-maligned "auto-tramps."

People still remembered the spit-and-bailing-wire rigs of the old twenties auto-tramps: tarpaper shacks on wheels, poorly balanced, poorly tired, overloaded, weaving and bouncing along some narrow road behind a weary Model T full of ragged, hungry-looking children, with a line of cursing motorists strung out in their wake, trying desperately to pass. Here were whole families begging and stealing and odd-jobbing around the country, living out their entire lives on the road. Not necessarily on their way *to* anywhere, most of them—simply on their way. The auto-tramps: directly descended, as a class, from the old-time wagon tramps and the houseboaters of a hundred rivers and streams—and all the homeless, hopeless wanderers of every age and time.

These were not exactly the role models that the thirties trailerite was seeking to emulate. But then, your typical thirties trailerites weren't really looking for role models or consciously imitating anyone. They were following their own survival instincts and indulging their rebelliousness and wanderlust a bit in the process, and that combination was leading them to blaze a brand-new social trail. They paid little attention to what journalists or trailer manufacturers or sociologists— or even the public at large—thought about what they were doing. For your typical thirties trailerite had, in Thoreau's words, "gone down to the woods for other purposes."

There is a certain type of American for whom freedom is more important than food. Always a minority, they reappear in every generation, right at the point where the social fabric is thinnest, right where the laws and mores and customs and taboos are just about to rupture and spill out into some new and temporarily looser mold: a new territory, a new social system, a new tomorrow. When Virginia got too crowded they left for Ohio; when they could see their neighbor's smoke, they left again, this time for Nebraska or Oregon. They were the frontier folk, the sod-busting pioneers. They crossed the Alleghenies afoot, just to by-God see what was on the other side. They went out to California in '49, not really for the gold—that was only an excuse— but for the journey itself, for the wildness and freedom of desert and mountain, for the pure shining infinite possibility of the West.

They're always on the road, spiritually if not physically, and their song is the road song and their literature is picaresque, the literature of the quest: *Moby Dick* and *Huckleberry Finn* and Kerouac's tales and *Henderson the Rain King* and *Blue Highways*.

They're always on the road, and so they always have plenty of company: drifters and vagabonds, migrants and transients, all the homeless and hopeless down at the bottom of the American social scale. They're not as put off by these people as you and I might be, because they're outsiders themselves. But they're not really of them, either, although at first glance they appear to be—and a first glance is all most of us give to passing strangers. You have to look carefully to see the difference: they're the ones who aren't dragging their feet. They're the ones marching to a private drum.

In many ways they are quintessentially American: the Daniel Boones, the Davy Crocketts, the strong and self-sufficient trail blazers. Always nonconformist, they're chafed by even the feather-light harness of democracy. Most people are satisfied to know exactly where the walls are; they want to know how high they are, as well. Most of us take comfort in simply knowing the rules; they're more interested in understanding the game. Theirs is the metaposition, the overview—not because they're smarter than the rest of us, but because they're more detached. Their ties to the social system are looser. They are a product of the system, but not quite a part of it. They're the observers, the outsiders, the misfits. If they appear rootless, it's because they're not entirely at home in our little neighborhood. Their allegiance is to some larger sphere: the continent, perhaps; or the race; or the planet. It may be that they only appear to be outsiders from our narrow point of view. It may be that they're perfectly comfortable, perfectly at ease—in the universe.

We can handle these misfits one at a time. Give them some blank paper and send them off to write *Walden* or *Let Us Now Praise Famous Men* or *Desert Solitaire* or *Pilgrim at Tinker Creek*. Sell them a few acres of rocks and tree stumps and let them found a commune like Amana or New Harmony or The Farm.

But what happens when they appear en masse? What happens when a quarter million or more of them come out of the woodwork at once, as they did in 1936? A quarter million self-sufficient individuals out there on the road, all marching in roughly the same direction, all following some hazy star of freedom and independence that's invisible to everybody else.

Does it help to pronounce them all sick with a strange new malady? Does it excuse them to say that they're not really rebels, misfits, cranks—that they just have a bad case of a recently isolated disease called trailer fever?

6 Trailer Fever

This living like bums or . . . gentleman tramps . . . suits us admirably.

—*letter to the editor,*
Trailer Topics,
January 1938

No insatiable restlessness is behind the movement. It is no gypsy inclination simply to move and keep moving at minimum expense. Climate is doubtless the primary cause—escape from winter's cold and from summer's excessive heat . . . escape from mortgages and the ownership of useless impedimentia—escape from conventionality with so many of its senseless requirements and prohibitions—escape from "keeping up with the Joneses."

—*Charles Edgar Nash,*
Trailer Ahoy! *1937*

We all have a little gipsy blood.

ad slogan for
1920s motorhome

Stanley and Dorena Ames live in a ten-by-sixty-foot Windsor, in one of the oldest trailer parks in Galveston, Texas. They don't refer to the twelve-ton Windsor, which they bought new in 1961, as a mobile home, although they're perfectly entitled to. It's wider than eight feet, and longer than the law allows: to take it on the highway requires a special tow vehicle and special permits in any state in the union. But to Stanley and Dorena their Windsor is a trailer, and they themselves are trailerites.

I've known them both since long before the Windsor was built. This entitles me to bait them a little.

"So when are you two going to settle down and buy a house?" I asked, last time I was in Galveston. I was sprawled full length on their full-length couch, facing Stanley in his ancient brown Strato-lounger. Behind him, maybe fifteen feet from the tip of my nose, Dorena puttered about in her kitchen.

She took the bait first, and her big Italian eyes flashed obsidian. "What in the world do we need of a house? *This* is more house than I can keep up with!" She waved a petite and perfectly manicured hand at their petite and perfectly manicured little world. Beyond the kitchen, a narrow hallway led off past bath and laundry and storage rooms, ending in the door to the master bedroom that seemed, to my eye, to be about a mile away. I spent the first fifteen winters of my life in three different trailers, every one of them small enough to park beneath the awning of this one. Simultaneously.

"When they start building houses the way this old Windsor's built, then I might buy one," Stanley rumbles from the Strato-lounger. "Show me a thirty-year-old tract house that doesn't have cracks and water-stains and five coats of peeling paint, inside and out. Take a look at those walls—that's the original finish, and it still shines like new!"

"The walls and ceiling could use a coat of wax," Dorena says apologetically. "I'm getting to be such a terrible housekeeper." I glance down to be sure my shoes aren't touching the couch. There might be cleaner rooms in Galveston—some of the surgical suites down at John Sealy Hospital, say—but I doubt it.

"This old rig's been through half a dozen hurricanes. There were some houses on this island didn't survive those storms." Stanley gives me a triumphant wink. "We had her hitched to the bobtail a couple of times, but we never did have to run."

"The bobtail"—a specially-built Ford hauler that pulled the Windsor to Galveston from North Carolina on their last move, back in the sixties—used to be parked out front. A few years ago they traded the bobtail for a mini-motor home, for vacations. I can see the mini out the picture window, shined and polished like the big blue Fairlane Dorena drives to work, and it occurs to me that if a trailerite owned

"Trailers have the emotional appeal of boats."
—*Fortune*, March 1937

"The only trouble is that, according to trailer 'addicts,' once you live in a home on wheels, you're never satisfied to be anchored to a permanent one again."
—*Popular Mechanics*, January 1937

nothing more than a single silver-plated spoon, he'd scour the silver off of it in a week.

"Can't you just see Stanley and me mowing the grass and painting the garage every Saturday? If we had a house and yard to keep up, it'd just be a mess. And so would we!" Dorena shakes her head. "I never understood why people want to be saddled with a big house and all that yard. Slavery's supposed to have been over with a hundred years ago!"

The Strato-lounger rumbles again. "If we decide to move, we can be outa here by noon. I know where I can get me another bobtail quick." I find myself grinning like a kid—there's that look in Stanley's eye, a look I hadn't seen since my father died. Defiance? Too strong. Smugness? That's closer. A quiet sense of independence, a knowledge that the world doesn't own you in quite the same way it does most people, that you actually could tell the boss to shove it. You probably won't, but you *could*. For a certain type of person, that sense of self-sufficiency, that feeling of control over your destiny, is worth far more than the family farm. *If we decide to move, we can be outa here by noon.*

Trailer fever.

My parents fell victim to it in '39 or '40, before I was born, and didn't recover until the mid-fifties. Stanley and Dorena bought their first rig in 1952, and they haven't recovered yet. Judging by the way they both rant at the word "house," the prognosis isn't good.

Trailer fever: the symptoms aren't so different, really, from the sort of madness that strikes the weekend sailor, the born-again yachtsman. It is no accident that over a dozen trailer companies, since 1928, have christened one of their models "The Land Yacht." Trailers and boats have a lot in common—not just in structure and function, but in their effects on the human psyche. Trailers and boats and full moons.

> "YACHT (yot) *n.* A hole in the water, surrounded by fiberglass, into which you pour money."
> —Popular saying, 1980s

One of the first recorded outbreaks of trailer fever occurred in New York City, in November of 1936, right under the watchful eye of a doctor of sociology from Penn State. It was the week of the National Automobile Show at Grand Central Palace. Three floors of seductively streamlined, fat-fendered new motorcars awaited their adoring public—three floors of split windshields and raked antennas, of black lacquer and nickel chrome. Heavy cloth banners draped the walls, floated down from the high ceilings. Soft music wafted through an atmosphere rich with the smell of cloth upholstery and paste wax and that faint, sweet, tingling odor of gasoline. Detroit has always known how to put on a show.

Tucked away up on the fourth floor—consigned to the attic, so to speak—was a modest trailer display, New York City's first. Forty camping trailers were scattered about the floor almost at random, little canvas and masonite road yachts, ranging in length from fifteen to twenty-six feet, in price from $450 for a bare-bones model to upwards of ten thousand dollars for one of the big brown Curtiss Aerocars.

The theme of the trailer display was "The Great Outdoors." Hastily painted wilderness scenes hung from the walls; cedar bark clung precariously to the huge Corinthian columns supporting the roof. A series of rustic wooden signposts announced the names of the twenty-five manufacturers present—romantic names like Aladdin and Palace and Kozy Coach and Covered Wagon; dying automotive names like Pierce-Arrow and Federal and Hayes; descriptive names like Auto Cruiser and Home-Mobile and Kabin-Coach.

These were the biggest names in the trailer industry in 1936, yet not one of these companies survives today. Almost all of them died before the war—some from poor management, some from the recession within the depression that began in late 1937, some from the material shortages caused by the defense build-up that preceded Pearl Harbor. Most, though, simply fell victim to the public backlash against the trailer that was already beginning—a backlash that ultimately expressed itself in hundreds of sour grapes editorials, in literally thousands of reactionary laws and regulations passed by cities and counties and states all across America.

But in November of 1936 these dark clouds were still below the horizon, and a kind of giggly, naive optimism pervaded the fourth floor of the Grand Central Palace. Arthur Sherman of Detroit, riding high as America's number one trailerman, called a press conference in his room at the Waldorf-Astoria to tell "the Covered Wagon story," and moved every company milestone back a year or two to bolster CW's newest ad slogan, "Originators and World's Largest Manufacturers of Trailer Coaches." All the other manufacturers took note, and chuckled, and moved their own company histories back appropriately, and a new trailer industry pastime, the game of "who was first," got quietly under way.

Was it slick, was it professional, was it high dollar, this first New York City trailer display? It was not. No matter; people flocked to the little wheeled homes by the thousands. Attendance, according to *The New York Times,* broke all records. "Getting into and out of the trailers seemed to fascinate many of the crowd," the *Times* noted.

Penn State sociologist Howard Roland was there playing sociologist—taking notes and making observations. Roland had spent the previous summer in a campground out in Colorado studying this curious new phenomenon, the house trailer. That was the summer of '36, the summer that trailers were suddenly everywhere: in the movies, on the radio, in newspaper cartoons and editorials, in washing detergent sweepstakes, in the display windows of Fifth Avenue department stores, and, of course, on the highways—especially those highways that led to Florida and southern California and the Rio Grande Valley of Texas.

Roland was not fooled by the watercolor wilderness on the Grand Central Palace walls. He had already begun to suspect that there was something more to this trailer fad than merely motor camping in a plywood tent:

> People filed past the shining new automobiles curious, eager and silent—but upstairs at the trailer show all was different. There was warmth, intimacy, no hurry. The curious stayed for hours, pondering their future in relation to homes, apartments, and mobile dwellings. It was an exhibit of human emotions and not one of streamlined steel and plywood. The trailers were incidental to the psychic contagion of the mart.

An exhibit of human emotions. What, exactly, were these curious and unhurried ponderers, these folk who stayed for hours at the trailer exhibit *seeing* in all that streamlined steel and plywood veneer? Were they really lulled by a painted forest and the smell of cedar bark into some sort of Arcadian reverie, hypnotized into a sudden nostalgia for the great outdoors? They came by the thousands to gawk, Roland tells us, and stayed by the hundreds to dream. What sort of dream was it that these little canvas-roofed doll houses inspired?

Of the twenty-five manufacturers who organized this first New York show, over half had gotten their start back in the motor-camping days, building tent-trailers and camping gear for the fresh-air-and-wood-smoke crowd—hence all that cedar bark and watercolor wilderness, all those paper mountains waving in the breeze. These manufacturers—and Arthur Sherman was foremost among them—thought they understood the trailer dream perfectly. They thought that trailer fever, the fanatical love at first sight that certain people seemed to feel for these strange little handcrafted vehicles, was easily explained: a lot of folk simply wanted to go camping in comfort.

Back to nature.

The song of the open road.

And they were partly right, of course. Thousands of people—especially in the first half of the thirties, before the real trailer mania set in—bought themselves a little house trailer strictly for vacations. Dragged it out to Yellowstone for two weeks in August, and slept in it every blessed night. Warm as toast. You bet. No worry about the bears. Having a wonderful time.

But what about the other fifty weeks of the year? A 1930s trailer that wasn't busy being an asset quickly proved to be a terrific liability. When not in use, it had to be not just parked, but stored—preferably indoors. Its little round bread-loaf roof was covered, not with metal, like today's travel trailers, but with canvas duck—that same pale, flimsy stuff that tents are made of. This canvas was sealed, on the way out the factory door, with a couple of hasty coats of aluminized paint. Leave it outside in the weather and that roof would need repainting twice, maybe three times a year. Without frequent waxing, the fancy red or black or brown or yellow leatherette on the trailer's sidewalls would quickly start to weather and crack. The windows and aluminum roof ventilators would leak. The tires would sun-rot. A garage or barn was almost a necessity for storing these early campers; exposed constantly to the elements, they required almost constant care.

And so, like motorboats and swimming pools and other low-use, high-maintenance toys, the trailer as camper never gained the widespread acceptance that the manufacturers hoped for during the thirties. There will always be a certain number of people who consider the upkeep on this kind of plaything to be worth it; most don't. After a few seasons, these early camping trailers began quietly changing hands, ultimately finding their way into the waiting arms of people with that contagion Dr. Roland spoke of—people who could see past the canvas and leatherette, the streamlined steel and paper-thin plywood, to the dream of freedom beyond. People with trailer fever.

"As for the difference in the mode of living, I can't see so much except we have less worries and after a while one takes on a more cheerful outlook on life."

"I see no reason to keep on working, grinding on and on till I die; I'm going to buy one of those trailer things, hitch it to my car, and my wife and I are going to take eight or nine months going to the Coast by way of Florida. . . ."

"I don't think I'll ever be content to go back to a regular house. We still have our furniture, but I suppose it will always be where it is now—in storage."

"We have lived in our trailer continuously for the past two and one-half years, in small towns, large cities, the country, the deserts, the mountains, in cold weather and in hot weather, in the North, the South and the West. This life becomes more interesting every day."

"One of the great beauties of trailer travel is the manner in which one completely shuts out the world when the curtains are drawn and the door closed. You may be camped in a parking lot in the heart of the roaring fifties in New York City, yet inside there is true home comfort."

"A trailer passed our store one day . . . and I said to my wife, 'Why not?' And she said to me, 'Why not?' And that was all. You know, twenty-five years in a shop without a vacation. So here we are."

"A trailer is fine for seeing our country economically—one gets the food he is accustomed to—meets many retired people—learns of things not often seen in books . . . and he always knows whose chin the blankets were pulled up under the night before."

"We went one summer to Macinac in a trailer. For my asthma. We liked it so well, I gave our house to my daughter and got free. That was four years ago."

"We had a choice—an old apartment or a modern trailer. Thank goodness we chose the trailer!"

These are some of the voices—long dead now—of the trailer pioneers of the 1930s, the folk who fell in love with their little flying flats and went off to live in them full-time. When you look at pictures of the trailers of that era, scalloped black-and-white photos over half a century old, it's not easy to understand what people saw in these primitive little vehicles. How small and cramped they were! Barely six feet wide inside, seldom over twenty feet in length, with crude gasoline cookstoves that looked, and smelled, and rattled in transit exactly like the little forest green Coleman stoves that people take to the woods today. (Many, in fact, were made by Coleman.) They had such diminutive sinks and lavatories—and toilets built for a race of pygmies. The typical trailer window of the period, sixteen inches by thirty-two inches, was little larger than a porthole, and most prewar models had only a single outside door, up front in the living room end. Almost all of these doors were five feet high or less, so that if you happened to forget to duck when you went in or out, you would remember in a flash.

Yet people stood in line to file through these little vehicles, stood in line to buy them. At one point in the 1936 season, Arthur Sherman's Covered Wagon Company was able to fill only one out of five of its orders. Dealers estimated they could have sold 200 to 300 thousand trailers that year; the major manufacturers, working at capacity, produced just over forty thousand.

Where was the magic in these little boxes?

Part of it lay in their very miniaturization, in what might be called the doll house effect. Any small copy of a familiar object has a fascination all its own: models of ships and trains and cars and airplanes, museum dioramas, toy soldiers, architects' models, midgets, babies, Statue of Liberty replicas, shrunken heads. Small may or may not be beautiful, but it is always and inherently interesting.

The first house trailers had this same fascination. They were apartments, cabins, bungalows—in miniature. Like their seagoing sister the

"We have grown up, yet most of us remember with—undisclosed—pleasure when we used to play house."
—*Trailer Topics,*
December 1937

yacht, they contained galleys and bedrooms and parlors complete in all their furnishings, but scaled down in size just enough to make them fascinating. People with absolutely no intention of ever owning a trailer still enjoyed peeking in the doors and windows of these little Alice in Wonderland homes, walking through them and marveling at their compactness, their neatness, their toylike quality.

Arthur Sherman and his family noticed this every time they took their first, primitive Covered Wagon out on the road back in 1929. Even when they were all inside the trailer, eating dinner or bedding down for a cozy night's sleep, strangers would come up and peer in the windows, or knock shyly on the door and ask to see inside. Sherman labeled these folk "trailer tappers." It was the trailer tappers—a constant stream of them, everywhere they went—that made Sherman decide to try marketing his little camper.

Trailer tapping was common all through the pioneer decade. The mid-thirties barrage of cartoons and newsreels and feature stories on the trailer, far from satisfying public curiosity about this new creation, seemed only to whet it. Science writer Edwin Teale noticed these legions of curiosity seekers in the Washington, D.C., municipal camp when he parked there briefly in the fall of 1936:

> Each afternoon, scores of visitors drove up and down the streets of the trailer park, looking over the different outfits and asking questions about prices and equipment. Trailer travelers, we found, are friendly folk, glad to help a fellow enthusiast.

Fortunately Teale didn't cross paths with the cantankerous Blackburn Sims, a transplanted Englishman who had published *The Trailer Home, with Practical Advice on Trailer Life and Travel* earlier that same year. "Do not leave the trailer unlocked," Sims warns his readers. "It seems that everyone in the known world wants to snoop in and around a trailer." He advises taking a firm stand against these uninvited guests:

> There are one million, five hundred and seventy-nine thousand, one hundred and three people in this country alone, by actual count, who seem to have nothing in the world to do but walk up to trailer doors with a silly smirk and say, "May we see your trailer?"
> They have various excuses—thinking of buying one—thinking of building one, etc. etc., ad infinitum.

Well, if they're thinking of buying one, the place to see them is in the show room. If they're thinking of building one, let 'em think.

Of course, if you want to be a party to this, go ahead and show your trailer. But, if you once start it, you will be overrun by a ravening hoarde.

Even in the Shirley Temple year of 1936, it seems, not every doll house had a doll in it.

Miniaturization—the doll house effect—may have drawn people to the trailer, but it's not the stuff that dreams are made of. What held them, what caused them to "stay for hours, pondering their future," was a whole constellation of dreams that this new creation evoked: the dream of home, the dream of newness, the dream of modernity, the dream of simplicity.

Brand-new, ultramodern, simplified home! Step right up and put your money on the table, folks! This is no mere camper! It's a brand-new, ultramodern, simplified *home*!

The trailer manufacturers of the thirties, with one or two exceptions, never really understood that what they were selling was not just a toy, but a new way of life. To them—practical, middle-aged males, for the most part, readers of *Popular Mechanics* and *The Saturday Evening Post*—the house trailer was merely a logical extension of the tent trailer, an improved camping device.

When they were confronted with the fact that some people were living full-time in their little creations, their usual reaction was simply to deny it—often at the top of their voice. Norman Christian Wolfe, the high-strung owner of Silver Dome, Inc., the number two trailer maker at mid-decade, dismissed the possibility of full-timers thus: "Apart from every other consideration, the lack of privacy and room would have the average family at one another's throats!" Our hero Arthur Sherman of Covered Wagon, whose five-child family was a bit more than average even in the thirties, kept insisting to the pack of reporters at his heels that "what we're mostly trying to sell is a vacation."

And yet, every November, when the new models came out, these trailer-coaches-that-were-not-houses got longer and roomier and warmer and better insulated—more houselike. This, the manufacturers

"Believe me, I'm glad to get back to our trailer. It's so much more comfortable than a stuffy apartment."
—Mrs. Vernon Kennedy, wife of Chicago White Sox pitcher, in *Trailer Topics,* June 1937

were quick to explain, was what their "vacation" customers seemed to want.

Brand-new, ultramodern, simplified home! Step right up. . . .

To move out of an old, drafty, mildewy house or apartment into a glossy, tight, hand-crafted little two-room flat that had just rolled, literally, off the assembly line; to put the very first coat of wax on a floor of inlaid linoleum; to open an icebox that smelled like new porcelain instead of old butter, an icebox that had yet to see a food stain; to cook the first meal on a shiny, factory-fresh, three-burner stovetop; to be surrounded by walls and ceiling of hand-rubbed birch, red oak, fir, bleached mahogany—this was the dream of newness.

To have at your fingertips the very latest in built-in gadgetry: a hot water heater, a six-tube radio (antenna wire cleverly hidden in the roof), a coaloil heating stove, an electric outlet in the living room for your iron and yet another in the kitchen for your toaster. To have on every easy to open window a tight brass screen to keep out insects. To have a toilet and shower in a miniature bathroom that you could scrub down, from floor to ceiling, in five minutes. To move, in one giant step, from an old house or flat into a new trailer—from the nineteenth century to the twentieth—here was the dream of modernity.

"No wonder the family man is taking the 'gypsy in him' for a ride. No wonder the nation envisages a revival of the covered wagon days to result, perhaps, in a novel type of resettlement in America."
—*Christian Science Monitor*, October 7, 1936

To be born, as almost every trailerite in the pioneering period had been, into a world of horse and buggy, of coaloil lamp and outside privy, and then, midway in the journey of your life, to find yourself the owner of a rickety two-story monster full of clanking plumbing and mysterious electric wires, a house heated by a huge, firebreathing machine in the basement that only an engineer could understand, a house continually in need of repairing and repainting and remodeling. To exchange all that complexity for a sleek, modern little wheeled bungalow with no secrets: open the cabinet under the sink and see all the plumbing, right down to the water heater. Fill the miniature furnace with coaloil (familiar smell!) and watch it drip, drip, drip into the burn chamber before you drop the match. To own—outright—a compact little home you could crawl over, climb under, tug about with the family car, a home you could be not merely owner but master of. Wasn't this the very dream of simplicity?

And yet the manufacturers of these brand-new, ultramodern, simplified homes didn't seem to understand, or simply refused to see, that

they were building something far different from an upgraded tent-
trailer. They refused to see that the old motor camper's dream—back
to nature, the song of the open road—didn't begin to explain the
phenomenon of trailer fever. They refused to admit that what a lot of
people were seeing in all that chrome and canvas and plywood was
not just a few warm and bug-free nights in Yellowstone, but a pioneer's
dream of a freer, more independent future. Not just a vacation, but a
whole new way of life.

"What in the world do we need of a house? This is more house than I
can keep up with!"

"If we decide to move, we can be outa here by noon."

"We had a choice—an old apartment or a modern trailer. Thank goodness we chose the trailer!"

7 Life in the Parks

It may be here noted that the trailerite practically lives out-of-doors.
—Professor Donald O. Cowgill, Mobile Homes, *1941*

Neighborliness pervaded the streets, and the faint memory of fried eggs.
—E. B. White, describing the Sarasota, Florida,
municipal trailer park, Harpers, *May 1941*

The journalists of the thirties and forties were endlessly fascinated by the nomadic aspects of this new way of living. Here were people from every walk of life, every state of the union, flowing in and out of these camps as smoothly as lava—thousands of ordinary Americans who had broken a lifetime of ties to become, almost overnight, at home on the highway. At home on the highway! The phrase had a romantic ring; it seemed to strike some deep bass note of yearning in the soul of readers and writers alike. It quickly became a cliché, popping up in newsreels, in magazine articles, in newspaper feature stories about these new American pioneers: whatever their background, whatever their roots, they were now a people at home on the highway. The phrase was utter nonsense, of course—a purely journalistic invention. Trailerites were no more at home on the highway than armadillos were. Trailerites were at home in their parks.

Not that the highway wasn't an important element in their mythology. Whether a familiar route or a strange one, the narrow, two-lane roads of the Depression were ribbons of adventure. Before interstates and airconditioning, cross-country car travel was a breezy kaleidoscope of the sights and sounds and smells of regional America. Every highway had its unique delights. Up in the rolling green tobacco country of northern Kentucky were tall, creosote-black curing barns that shouted

"At Lordsburg take the shortcut to Benson, Ariz. This route is part gravel but I have always found it good."
—"Trailer Route to California," *Trailer Topics,* December 1937

85

Even the nicest prewar trailers, like this Vagabond, had limited interior space and no artificial cooling, so a good part of daily life—eating, reading, entertaining—took place on the patio.

CHEW MAIL POUCH TOBACCO and SEE SEVEN STATES FROM ROCK CITY in huge block letters on their sides. Down in the Mississippi delta, where the cotton fields lay treeless and still under a noon haze, the thick, lazy air was always faintly sweet with insecticide dust from the little yellow biplanes that hummed like hornets over the landscape. Rolling westward through the endless wheat fields of Kansas and Colorado, you watched for the exact minute when the shimmering white cumulus clouds that lay across the horizon would change, quite suddenly and miraculously, into the snow-capped tops of the Rockies—a metamorphosis that never failed to delight.

The highway led everywhere, and so of course it was romantic, constantly beckoning. But the trailerite was never at home on it. The highway was a means rather than an end: not a place in itself, it was simply the route you took to some new place. The highway was always there, waiting, whenever you were ready to roll.

Ready to roll!

In our family the decision usually came on Thursdays, at the supper table, a drop-leaf affair that popped up, for meals and letter writing and homework, between the kitchen and living room. My dad, the tanned, wiry, gray-moustached wagon master in bricklayer's khaki, would make the announcement, his voice casual, almost tentative: the job was winding down, he was thinking of drawing his time tomorrow, before the layoffs start. Would anybody object if we planned to roll out Saturday morning? ("Roll out"—my favorite words! Red neon goes zipping up and down my spinal column!) Emily (her voice also casual: there's a power play going on here, but they're both enjoying it) points out that I have a book report due on Monday, and she has some dry cleaning out. A brief discussion, then a mutual conclusion: they can pick the dry cleaning up on the way out of town. "What about your book report?" the wagon master would ask, and my grin was answer enough.

Turn in your schoolbooks, pay your library fines, pick up your interim report card, always straight A's. School was as easy as life; life was as easy as making friends; and making friends, in those innocent times, was as easy as leaving them:

"Where you movin to?"

"I dunno—California, Texas, someplace where you can't see your breath."

"Luck-eee!"

Always one step ahead of the weather: leave the midwest sometime between the last leaf and the first snowflake, arrive on the Gulf Coast in the wake of the season's final hurricane. To practice his bricklaying trade—to create fireplaces, walls, entire buildings out of ancient clay and water—my father needed, or at least preferred, good weather. I came to expect it. It was an idyllic life for a child—barefoot all year long. If not, move on. One winter it rained too much in Los Angeles; we left for Tucson. A third of a century later, I still have no patience with ice and snow, or even a chilly north wind. Both evoke an old

"There is also . . . a curious sense of poignancy which is lent to trailer-camp life by the awareness that before long you'll be leaving. It's the same thing that makes a man's life seem more sparkling in a war, simply because he may shortly lose it."
—James Jones, author of *From Here to Eternity*

"the oft-repeated expression, 'north in the summer and south in the winter.'"
—*Trailer Topics*, May 1940

instinct: pack up, hitch up, roll out. There's an empty space waiting on a park somewhere, in full sunshine—the epicenter of a bright, mysterious, friendly new world.

"They haven't ever lived in a real house, but goodness me, they've surely been more places than most kids in America, I bet!"
—Mrs. Richard F. Vale, mother of four, *Trailer Topics,* May 1939

Despite the fears of the sociologists, the handwringing about rootlessness, they were wonderful places to grow up, the parks. This was the mid to late forties, a war away from the pioneers who had carved out a place for the house trailer in the American social wilderness. But trailer life and trailer parks had changed surprisingly little in those ten turbulent years. The basic elements of the trailerite life, forged by the pioneers in the thirties, continued almost uninterrupted through the war and right into the early fifties.

This was at least partly because the trailers themselves changed so little until well after the war. From roughly 1935 to 1948, they remained one- or two-room affairs, six to eight feet wide, around twenty feet in length. With so little living space inside, much of daily life naturally took place outside: washing and ironing and gossip, peeling shrimp and snapping beans, reading the paper, tying flies, visiting, playing canasta. Small wonder that the trailerites of the thirties and forties so often gravitated to the South, to the Gulf states of Florida, Alabama, Mississippi, Louisiana, Texas. Park life was richer and more communal down there where the weather was milder. The better parks—the all-year parks that could afford to put in more amenities—were more numerous there.

In the better parks, every trailer space had its own patio, or deck: wood planks, concrete, sometimes just cinders or gravel. And over every patio the trailerite would erect his pastel-striped awning—blue and white, green and white, red and white. The awnings gave trailer life a circusy feel: they were like a little piece of the Big Top right over your front door, coloring your complexion, coloring your mood, coloring the very air you breathed. As soon as you got the awning up, and tied the dog or hung out the canary—everybody traveled with either a dog or a canary—you began to consider the patio as part of your house. You set a card table out there and ate supper in the long twilight, flyswatter in one hand and fork in the other, waving one of the two at everyone who walked by.

The people of the parks were always afoot, day and night, like forest animals—out crunching the gravel with their sandals, their bedroom slippers, their bare feet. Someone always going to the washrooms, going to the store, going up to the park office to make a phone call, going next door to borrow a match, going over to row 4 to flirt. Kids played up and down the "drives," the broad streets that separated the rows of back-to-back trailers. Cars came and went, residents and visitors and the merely curious, picking their way carefully around potholes and tricycles and dogs and children, parking wherever they stopped—and stopping wherever they chose.

Cars were the park sculpture, the sculpture I grew up with, the only sculpture I knew as a child. Big cars they were: Detroit iron. (Throughout my childhood my dad drove nothing but Chryslers—old Walter P. was one of his heroes. I should have known he was losing interest in life when, just before he died, he traded down to a midsized Dodge.) Oldsmobiles—Rocket 88s and 98s—were popular on the parks. They had the size and power (and the prestige, don't forget the prestige, it was as important as carburetion) for trailer pulling. And there were cars from the gone world, too: Studebakers, Hudsons, DeSotos, and big black humpbacked Nashes, always hot to the touch.

Most of these cars were surprisingly new, for this was after the war, and even though auto prices had doubled between 1941 and 1946, money was still easier than it had been in the thirties. The trailerites, so recently evolved from the hardy old auto-campers, the tin canners, adored their automobiles. They would spend hours discussing them, polishing them, tuning and tweaking them to get a little smoother idle or a little better mileage, spend evenings and weekends jacking them up, putting on new shocks, tightening the hitch, adjusting the brakes. To service your own car—change oil and plugs, set the timing— seemed natural then, and it still does to me: a small source of satisfaction, power, independence.

Independence—within the framework of community—was a major value on the trailer parks, where values, like daily life, went unhidden. Cars represented independence, as did the trailers themselves: "We can be outa here by noon." A twenty-five- or fifty-cent hike in the rent, a neighbor cooking with too much garlic, a dirty restroom—anything or nothing was reason enough to move. This fickleness on the part of the

"Automobile repairs and oil changes are strictly forbidden in the park, except in space provided by the management."
—regulation #23, Mother's Trailer Park, Toledo, Ohio, 1939

trailerite made park owners uneasy: a backed-up sewer, a brief power outage, a single obnoxious Saturday night party might trigger a mass exodus, leave them with an empty park by noon.

Laws were passed during the thirties to prevent trailerites from removing their wheels, but these laws were directed at a different class of trailer dweller, a minority within a minority—the immobile poor. Nobody, in my memory, ever thought of pulling the wheels off his rig. Put jacks under the corners, of course, to stabilize her so she wouldn't shake when you walked about inside. But leave those wheels in place, ready. And go out and pump the tires up every once in a while—it keeps the managers on their toes.

Neatness and order were strong trailerite values, too. Because housekeeping was comparatively easy, there seemed no excuse for slovenliness. Also there wasn't room for it. Everything had its place in a trailer. Leave it out, leave it just lying around, and you fell over it—or worse yet, someone else did. The rule, at least in our household, was simple: take it out, use it, put it away. When you dirty a dish, you wash it—immediately. Magazines go in the magazine rack, coats and purses in the closet, shoes under the bed. Even the biggest trailers were notoriously short of horizontal space. Every table and shelf and cabinet top had multiple daily functions. There was simply no time for them to accumulate clutter.

Neatness and order: all part of the genetic structure that made you susceptible to the disease of trailer fever, made you a natural trailerite—one of *them*. You can see it in Dorena Ames's immaculate living room, in Stanley's trig little Dodge motor home parked out beside the patio. But on the parks of the thirties and forties, neatness was mostly an indoor value. Outside, all was chaos. Kids played everywhere, with little sense of the distinction between my yard and your yard. Kids aren't neat unless they have to be, even trailer kids. They just naturally spread chaos: toys and rocks and boards and bottles and birdfeathers, and fifty nifty things salvaged out of somebody's trash.

Down under the trailer, down in those deep, cool shadows behind the wheels, seemed like a natural place to stash certain things, natural for adults and children alike—a kind of substitute basement. Rules had to be made about such storage: nothing beneath the coach, everything in the storage sheds provided by the management. Even in the best

"Don't let your hitch get rusty."
—saying in the parks, 1940s

"It is my opinion that trailers appeal particularly to persons of a neat turn of mind."
—E. B. White, *Harpers,* May 1941

parks, this rule was hard to enforce. What to do with that carton of pop bottles you'll be taking back to the store on Saturday, that cracked canoe paddle that only needs a few minutes to repair?

Keeping the space under the trailers tidy was a daily battle for the conscientious park manager, a battle that must have felt something like the Hundred Years' War. Peace didn't come until the fifties, when trailers finally ceased their roaming, and the better parks began requiring skirts of metal or wood around the bottoms of the coaches. A skirt blocked the north wind and made the trailer's floor warmer. A skirt hid the wheels and utility connections, and gave the park an aura of semipermanence. But mostly, a skirt removed the ever-present temptation to toss certain items down into that inviting darkness "just for a day or two."

The old parks, before underground utilities, were a snarl of wires. Electric lines and loudspeaker wires and makeshift radio antennas swung from tree to tree in long arcs, like the trajectories of apes. Impromptu clotheslines—always full—zig-zagged back and forth between A to B. (Those big-armed women who erected them had a marvelous sense of physics—who ever saw one break?) And taut awning guys, to hold up all those circus stripes between windstorms. On the ground were water pipes and spigots, drain hoses and garden hoses and dog chains, miniature picket fences around miniature flowerbeds containing miniature white wooden wheelbarrows.

All this was the milieu of daily and nightly games of tag, kick the can, cops and robbers, steal-sticks, war. In a trailer park, to be an active child was to be a nimble child—or break your teeth. Chaos was everywhere. All the more need, then, for order *inside* the trailer, all the more need for running a tight ship: take it out, use it, put it away.

They were wonderful places to grow up, those old parks. Every trailer held a kind of surrogate parent, and there was a trailer—two trailers, actually, back to back—every thirty feet. Somebody was always making cookies, shelling pecans, organizing a trip to the dime store or the woods or the lake or the beach. Bakers brought home day-old bear claws and distributed them with a wink to the park kids, right before supper. Old bachelor accountants with passes to the company swimming pool would loan them to your mom, just for a smile. Lots of people around, people of all ages, to teach a kid to carve boomerangs,

> "Every guest must keep his parking space clean and free from waste and rubbish at all times."
> —Mother's Park regulation #8

Although moralists attacked trailer life for its lack of privacy, the parks, with their small town sense of security and a surrogate parent in every trailer, were wonderful places for children.

make kites, play guitar, string a fishing pole, build a slingshot—right out on their patios.

Not that there was no privacy, no sense of territory. Every trailer had an outside door, and a wood frame screen door just behind it. When the weather was nice, the outside door was almost always fastened open, snapped back flush to the side of the trailer, leaving the screen door—with its little plywood sliding panel, its "trap door" that allowed access to the doorlatch from inside the trailer—exposed. (That sliding panel was great for handing small objects like cookies in or out without opening the screen door and letting in flies. Or for standing up on the trailer step and talking to the kid inside, nose to nose.)

But if the weather was nice and the outside door was shut, that usually meant the people had gone off somewhere, or didn't want to be bothered. If the outside door was shut, the polite thing to do was to stop at the edge of the patio and bellow, Kentucky-fashion: "Hello the house!"

A communal lifestyle; a comforting environment for a child. Eyes everywhere watching you, though. Got to keep your nose clean—or know your neighbors: Mrs. Garrett across the street won't blab, but ol' lady Hawkins next door will. If it's devilment you have in mind—and what kid doesn't?—then you'd better wait till dark. The night belongs to children, anyway.

Adults operated under the same eyes; they, too, had to wait till dark. The parks were full of small town hypocrisies, small town values, because they were small towns. Every park would have a few residents who were almost permanent—the ones with the picket fences and flower gardens, the old-timers. These were the guardians of the flame, the park's moral standard-bearers. One of them would visit you when you pulled in—check you out, let you know the rules:

"Things generally get pretty quiet here after nine-thirty or ten."

"I don't suppose you folks are drinkers? People here don't go in for a lot of drinkin' and carryin' on . . ."

Words to the wise. People who didn't fit didn't stay.

There were high-class (read: working-class) parks and low-class parks—not much in between. The guardians of the flame, the moral standard-bearers, saw to that. What these permanent residents would tolerate became the park norm. (Dorena Ames: "We didn't stay long at that park. The people in the trailer behind us never shut their curtains when they changed clothes!" Stanley: "They were low-life!")

In the parks, sociability was important: holding your own in informal chat, called "visiting" or "neighboring." Not heavy-duty sociability, mind—not palsy-walsy. The age of community dances, of parkwide potlucks, was past; it died with the war. That kind of solidarity, group spirit, us-against-them, belonged to a smaller group of trailerites, a more select group: the pioneers of the thirties. This was the forties, the Age of Chat; a transition stage. The Age of Impersonality was coming. Television and airconditioning were coming to seduce everyone inside, glue them to the couch, make them forget the pattern of the stars in

"If this camper's rockin, Ain't no use in knockin."
—bumper sticker, 1980s

"Improper exposure, excessive use of intoxicating liquor, immoral conduct will result in the immediate expulsion of the offender from the park."
—Mother's Park regulation #13

"If people wanted to raise hell, they wouldn't go to a trailer camp."
Ollie Trout, Miami park owner, 1936

Cassiopeia, the smell of the evening breeze, the names of their neighbor's cousins out in Iowa. Make them forget how to visit, how to just *be* with one another: how to sit, in the shadowy twilight, for two, three, five minutes or more between the last remark and the next. Evenings were longer then, and the night air milder. Time itself had a different flavor.

Wonderful places to grow up, those old parks. They were my cradle and my kindergarten, the soil and sunshine of the endless summer of my childhood. It's not easy to write about them; I left my heart in the parks, thirty-odd years ago, and I've been trying to wing it with just my head ever since.

The American trailer park evolved, quite naturally and organically, out of the old auto-camp of the twenties motor gypsies. Camping trailers—like Sherman's little nine-foot box, like the Auto-Kamp and the Coleman and the Gilkie and the Clare and a dozen other fold-up canvas rigs—helped ease the transition, for they'd been showing up at the campground gates in increasing numbers since the late teens. The earliest ones were homemade, and some were surprisingly sophisticated. Even the crudest twenties tent-trailer demanded a 110-volt hook-up for lights, toasters, irons. By 1930, trailer campers were beginning to ask for hose connections to feed their built-in plumbing systems as well.

Camp operators shouldn't have been surprised. Motor homes (they still went by house-car or palace car or camper car in the twenties and thirties) had been carrying water about in pressurized tanks since before World War I. But of course a motor home could drive over to the spigot whenever it needed a refill; whereas these cocky little automobile trailers were parking and unhitching and then demanding that the water be piped out to them.

Change came slowly, as needed. A camp operator might run water to one small area, and direct the rigs with inside plumbing to park there, charging a bit more for the privilege. As demand grew, the water lines could be expanded, a few lots at a time. Eventually, business permitting, the entire camp would have running water without a big lump sum outlay—without the owner having to go into debt.

Then came the demand for sewer hook-ups. At first these were only

---

"Here in the small camp there are no recreation facilities, indeed nothing at all to assist the populace to spend their leisure hours, except 'neighboring.'"
—Donald O. Cowgill,
Mobile Homes, 1941

"Would you like to go in business for yourself—perhaps get into something requiring only a small amount of capital and promising a reasonable return? Then start a trailer camp."
—*Popular Mechanics*,
April 1937

for the kitchen and lavatory sinks, an easy trick: Just knock both ends out of a fifty-five-gallon drum and bury it upright, under the sink drain. Fill it with rocks and gravel, and let the sink water percolate down through it and out the bottom and back into the earth—provided, of course, that the soil is sufficiently porous, and the local health authorities approved, which they usually did.

Toilets were another matter. Toilets were big time sewage, a pain in the gluteus for everyone concerned. Bathtubs—little galvanized two-by-four-footers, about fourteen inches deep—actually beat flush toilets into many of the early trailers, hiding under beds or dinette seats, because tub water is "gray" water, and relatively easy to dispose of. But toilets—what to do about toilets? The simplest option, and the cheapest, was to leave them out of the trailer entirely: make the trailerites use the washrooms in the camps.

Unfortunately, people demanded toilets. "That rig got a bathroom?" was the question most often asked of trailer salesmen and of new arrivals in camp. There was status in being able to answer in the affirmative: "You bet!" But so few of the thirties camps had toilet hook-ups that a lot of trailerites who spent the extra money for bathroom-equipped rigs found themselves using the little closet-sized room mostly for storage, and falling in line at the camp's public washroom right along with everyone else.

A compromise solution was the dry toilet, nothing more than a wooden box with a toilet seat on top and a slop bucket hidden inside—a kind of indoor outhouse. The slop bucket had to be periodically hauled off to the bathhouse for dumping and cleaning, an unsavory task that smacked a little too much of the bad old days before indoor plumbing—days that most of the early trailerites could remember all too well. Barring sickness or debility, everyone in the prewar camps used the public facilities, and gladly.

That's why there was surprisingly little protest when, in April of 1938, the city of Los Angeles passed a regulation making the use of public restrooms in parks mandatory: "No trailer toilet," the ordinance read, "may be used within the city under any circumstances." Only one of a thousand such antitrailerite laws—laws that were, prima facie, discriminatory and unconstitutional—the Los Angeles ordinance was never seriously challenged until well after the war. The local trailer

"There has never been a satisfactory toilet designed for trailers . . . there are various chemical commodes and other devices, but none of them are satisfactory to the fastidious."
—*Trailer Topics*, April 1939

Community halls and washrooms were the hubs of trailer park life in the thirties, just as they had been for the tin canners a decade before.

"It may seem far-fetched, but I have found remark-able friendships over the washtub."
—Laurene T. Cork, *Trailer Topics,* June 1939

manufacturers, whose products were mostly lightweight camping rigs without toilet facilities, saw it as a kind of protective tariff against the elephantine trailers from "back East." And the local trailerites made little protest; like their eastern counterparts, they were already accustomed to queuing up at the washrooms, towels on their shoulders and soap clutched tightly in their hands.

This made the park washrooms social hubs—places where everyone met their neighbors on a more or less regular basis. Shaving beside a man in a common mirror morning after morning at least builds camaraderie, if not friendship. When you bump into him again the next fall, in a park out in Seattle—same face, same trailer, new car—then for sure it's time to exchange names, trade come-by-for-coffees. Who knows—if the spark is there, you could become friends, even old friends. My mother, a rather shy and reserved person by trailerite standards, died in 1983, still trading annual Christmas letters with a dozen people she'd met in the parks. She hadn't lived in a trailer park for twenty-nine years.

After the war, people stopped naming their trailers. Many still placed big cards in the front window, beside the ice card and the milk card, that carried their own names and their city and state of origin: The Wilkinsons—Bob and Betsy—Milwaukee, Wisconsin. (In mobile home parks today some people still continue this tradition.) But by the forties, few trailerites took the trouble to hand-letter some folksy-cutesy nickname across the bow of their little land yacht, the way so many of the thirties pioneers had done—names like "Our Wandering Wigwam," "Dew Drop Inn," "The Canvas Castle," or "Aftermath" (a retired algebra teacher from Iowa).

Even the earliest factory-built trailers, like cars and airplanes before them, carried their company logos in some conspicuous place: on a tin plate beside the door, centered on the front or rear of the coach, or emblazoned across the chrome hubcaps. But Aladdin or Airfloat, Elcar or Travelodge, Land-Cruiser or Liberty or Stream-Lite were simply too generic, too impersonal, too common for the trailerites of the thirties. They had to add their own touch to their coaches: "The Loose Caboose," "Charlie's Folly," "Hoosier Friend."

This tradition of christening your trailer, of personalizing it, grew out of the home-built era of the twenties, when people who craved a house trailer had to hammer it together themselves—unless they had a minimum of five thousand dollars (equivalent today to something like $100 thousand) to shell out for one of Glenn Curtiss's sleek, vinyl-clad Aerocars. People who build things from scratch—a rowboat, a vacation cabin, a custom car—get a lot of time and ego involved in the project, and seem to feel compelled to give it some sort of clever moniker. It's almost a duty. My wife and I live in an unusual-looking solar house that we designed and built ourselves, and every second person who sees it asks "What do you call it?" Our house, we tell them—we call it our house. The answer almost never satisfies.

"The trailer has become for many trailerites a hobby. They are constantly planning alterations."
Donald O. Cowgill, *Mobile Homes*, 1941

The prewar parks, the pioneer parks, tended to be smaller and friendlier and more democratic than the parks of the late forties. During the war and just after, thousands of families were forced into trailer life by circumstance: housing shortages, money shortages, imagination shortages. Many of these newcomers simply didn't want to be there. Many were in a holding pattern, just waiting for a chance to move into a "real" house or apartment. Their presence altered the atmosphere of the parks somewhat. Before the war, almost everybody in the better parks was there by choice. Before the war, the spirit of adventure, the awareness of sharing a new experiment in living still prevailed; trailer people were friendly to one another out of a sense of uniqueness and common purpose, much as vacationing tent campers are today.

The tone for the thirties parks had been set by the tin can tourists, a decade earlier: your friends are my friends, and my friends are your friends. And the early park managers did their best to keep this camaraderie rolling. They put an incredible amount of energy into the organizing of fish fries and ice cream socials and dances and bridge clubs and horseshoe tournaments and ball games and group sings and band concerts and plays and lectures—and anything else they could come up with to get people out of their trailers, get them to mix. The managers saw this as part of their job: keeping the camp atmosphere thick and sociable. This was especially true in the Florida parks, the "play" parks, where vacationers and retirees were likely to outnumber the working people. Today, not everyone would want to come home from a day's work, or even a day's fishing, and face an invitation to an all-neighborhood taffy pull. But in the thirties, in the parks, a surprising number of people would change their clothes, grab a bite to eat, and go off to the clubhouse to pull taffy with the neighbors.

In many parts of the country, community kitchens were common in parks before the war. These were carry-overs from the motor camping decade and had largely disappeared by the forties. As alien as it now seems, many of the pioneers thought no more of sharing a common kitchen with strangers than they did of sharing a laundry tub, for the very good reason that cooking a big meal in warm weather could turn a house trailer into an oven, and only trailers in the land yacht class—Curtiss Aerocars and their imitators—had any sort of cooling beyond a small electric fan or two. Screened doors and windows for cross-ventilation were standard items, along with screened ventilators

"These trailer park operators know the traveler will stay longer if he is made to feel part of the community."
—*Trailer Topics,*
July 1940

"TRAILER CAMP DELUXE—6 mi. from Palm Springs on Indio Highway. Electric connections, toilets, shower baths, city water, piped to each trailer space. Gas stoves. 50¢ per night. $2.50 week and $8 month. Grocery store & post office nearby."
—classified ad,
Trailer Travel,
October 1936

Before airconditioning, the only difference between hot and miserably hot was an electric fan. The better parks, like this one in Childersburg, Alabama, provided lots of shade and green grass.

in the roof to siphon off ceiling heat, but there was no artificial cooling. (By 1936 the Statler Hotel in St. Louis was advertising airconditioning in three hundred of its rooms, the first hotel in America to provide refrigerated air on such a grand scale. And in '38 a couple of the major midwestern trailer manufacturers, Indian and Schult, began offering refrigeration units as an expensive option. But airconditioning didn't become common in house trailers—or, for that matter, in American houses—until the fifties.)

So the first requirement of a good trailer park in the thirties and forties was shade. With a ceiling only inches above the top of your head—six-foot-three was the average interior height of a prewar trailer—you needed a great, sprawling tree between your roof and the sun if you hoped to stay cool down the long afternoon. Without shade, a house trailer could get as hot as a tent. A common practice in the desert parks of southern California, where trees, sprawling or otherwise, were scarce, was to erect the awning over trailer and patio both, leaving an air gap of a foot or so above the roof for circulation. This worked best if you remembered not to cover the stove vent; otherwise you could burn up an awning, and possibly your trailer with it, when you fired up to cook the first meal.

Shade was so important that the cleverest park owners tried to work some implication of it into their camp names: Torrey's Shady Court, Bell's Shady Grove, Pine Oak Auto Park, Maplewood Auto Camp. Others coined slogans for their business cards: "There's always a breeze 'neath shady trees," "Seventy-six shaded sites with grass and flowers," "An orange tree for every trailer." (This last from a camp in Florida? In California? No—in the Rio Grande Valley of Texas.) Even the Gulf Coast parks—the beachside parks of Bermuda grass and sandburrs, those play parks where you could almost always count on an ocean breeze—found they needed shade trees (small palms would do) to draw a loyal and long-term clientele.

"Shaded grassy plot for every trailer."
—ad for Ollie Trout's in *Trailer Topics*, April 1939

Word traveled fast among the early trailerites: which park in town offered the lowest rates, the best landscaping, the cleanest washrooms, the most entertainment or the quietest Saturday nights. Word of mouth was still the park owner's best advertising before the war, for the old auto-camper grapevine was alive and well throughout the thirties, and friends drew friends to their favorite parks. One of my parents' twice-told tales concerns meeting some former neighbors, a couple about their age, on the ferry into Galveston one fall. The neighbors spotted my folks' LaSalle and Schult, and came over to welcome them back. "Where you planning to stay?" they asked.

"Murdochs," my dad told them. It was the park they had stayed in for two winters running, the park where the couples had first met.

"Oh, don't go to Murdochs, it's gone downhill," they said. "Come on up to Miramar with us!" So my parents followed them to Miramar, twelve blocks further west along the seawall, and two weeks later a hurricane swept in off the Gulf and wiped out every trailer in Murdochs. Miramar had only minor damage.

Word of mouth—it could work for you or against you if you were

In the poorer camps, like this one near San Diego, there was no paving or land-scaping, and the prime requirement for a trailer park—shade—was missing. During the war such parks became common.

a camp owner. As the thirties wore on, more and more people went into the trailer park business, and the competition grew keener. Newer parks raised the ante on older parks (Completely tiled restrooms! Electric washing machines!) and emptied them of their brightest and best. The older trailers—and the uglier home-builts—stayed behind. Old rigs attract old rigs, new rigs attract new. Thus even before the war the sifting out, the stratifying, of the great wheeled democracy began, so that it became possible to say, by the late forties, by my time in the parks, that there were high-class parks and low-class parks, and not much in between.

Not that class distinctions—snobbery—had ever been entirely absent within the trailer movement. The American Municipal Association, surveying the trailer situation in fifty-three cities during the summer and fall of 1936, found trailer dwellers who made a clear distinction between those who merely camped and "those who camped and hung out their wash." One Charles Edgar Nash, the author of *Trailer Ahoy!*, an introductory book on trailering published in 1937, admits a preference for small camps over large, because they "tend to be neater in appearance [and] unsightly wash is not flying every day in the week."

What is it about hanging wash that disturbs people so? Is it a prud-

"Those who have the cheaper trailers are known as tin-can tourists; those who have the elaborate ones are veritable land yachtsmen."
—editorial, *The New York Times*, August 8, 1936

ishness about underwear? A subconscious fear of ghosts—of unten-
anted garments that leap and dance on the invisible breeze? Or do we
see our own death foreshadowed in these empty pants and shirts and
dresses? Why should something as familiar as our clothing, freshly
baptized and hung in the sun to dry, offend us so?

Drury College professor Donald Cowgill spent the summers of '38
and '39 dragging his family about the country in a newly purchased
top of the line Palace Travel Coach, filling the rig's miniature bathtub
with notes for a book on the sociology of trailering—a book that the
University of Pennsylvania published in 1941. A magnanimous fellow,
Cowgill: in 127 pages of observations, he never once mentions the
wash. What he does mention, though, is a kind of segregation or stra-
tification within the parks, based on three criteria: length of stay, condition of the coach, and presence or absence of children. Cowgill's
categories ring true to my own park experience, a decade later.

Overnighters, Cowgill noted, or people who were staying less than
a week, always got the least desirable lots: the ones with no shade, the
ones with poor drainage, the ones just a bit too convenient to the
washrooms. Overnighters weren't exactly ignored by the regular residents—unfriendliness among trailerites was a sin—but they usually
weren't singled out and made to feel as welcome as someone pulling
into one of the more permanent lots would be. (Even in a transient
society, you could still be too transient to fit in.)

My cocky little bow-legged father stubbornly refused to make this
distinction; he would as soon spend the evening chatting with total
strangers, people whom he might never see again, as with friends. This
made him a bit of an eccentric in park society, but only a bit. When
people saw him dragging a chair over to some overnighter's patio they'd
shake their heads philosophically and say, "Well, looks like old Dave's
out there running for mayor again."

Fewer than half of the trailer families Cowgill surveyed had kids
aboard, and he noted that those trailers with children were usually
grouped toward the back of the park, away from what he calls the
"gold coasters"—retired folk, for the most part, and conspicuously well
off—whose expensive rigs always adorned the front rows to make the
park look more attractive than it usually was. Cowgill observed that

these gold coasters didn't seem to associate freely with the rest of the trailerites, and he attributes this behavior to economic differences, but I suspect that children were a more significant factor than he suggests. People in the process of child raising usually have more in common with other parents than with childless couples and retirees. And people beyond childbearing age don't always welcome the permanent presence of children. Part of a kid's initiation to each new park was to learn which trailers you could play around and which you couldn't.

If we could climb into the basket of a balloon and float over a typical pioneer trailer park on some calm, clear morning of, say, 1939, if we could ascend quietly to five hundred or a thousand feet, hovering low enough to hear conversations on the ground, yet high enough to see trailer life steadily and see it whole, if we could look down godlike on this microcosm of post-Depression, prewar America, what would we see? An orderly grid of streets, little different from any other subdivision, streets eighteen to twenty feet wide surfaced with dull black macadam, perhaps, or with gravel, or—if our park happened to be near the Gulf, in Tampa or Pascagoula or Corpus Christi, say—with "Gulf Coast gravel," a coarsely ground oyster shell dredged up from nearby bays and estuaries, chalk white and glaring in the sun.

The trailers themselves would be almost as carefully ordered as the streets: two rows back to back inside each block, their hitches all pointing out, their bright, painted aluminum roofs looking like so many foil-covered Easter eggs. Each sits on a twenty-five-by-thirty-foot lot, though the lot lines are no more visible from our balloon than they are on the ground, for fences—except the small ones around flower plots—are nonexistent, and any division of properties is accomplished with shrubbery, if at all. (The number one park on the East Coast, Ollie Trout's Camp in Miami, had a palm tree at every lot corner.) Occasionally you may spot an empty lot, looking like the hole left by an extracted tooth. Nothing marks it but a rectangle of patio, a dark dot where the sewer juts up waiting for a trailer drain, and, toward the back, a short power pole with a meter on it. The better parks, by the late thirties, had all gone to individual electric hookups. In the flat-rate parks people always complained of being overcharged for current: "We don't hardly use any juice at all, and yet they bill us the same thirty-

"Modern, 10 acres, paved streets, grass lots, shade, clean rest rooms, plenty hot water, no dogs, adults only."
—postcard ad for Westland Trailer City, Long Beach, California, 1943

five cents a week they do the Frazier's—and you know how much electricity those people use!")

Except for the overnighters, most of the trailers in the park will have an awning, eight or ten feet wide and running almost full-length down the curb side of the coach, covering the front door, the entire patio, and then some. If it's a poor park, a hardscrabble park, there won't be a tree or a shrub or a blade of grass anywhere, and the family jalopy will probably be pulled right up beside the trailer, where the patio's supposed to be. In a poor park the awning, if there is one, will cover the car, without much consideration for living space around it. (Ollie Trout's had grass everywhere you looked, and a park attendant backed your trailer in for you and hooked up the utilities, and you parked your car in a marked space out on the wide, paved drive in front of your rig.)

Even from a thousand feet up, you can see many of the contradictions inherent in the trailerite life. Look: they've chosen to live in small, discrete, self-sufficient family units on wheels. Obviously they value their independence, their autonomy. Yet here they are, by the dozens—by the hundreds, even—jammed into a regimented mass, their little homes never more than fifteen feet from each other, their windows on three sides looking right into those of their neighbors. (Why weren't the lots laid out in parallelograms instead of rectangles, so each trailer sat on a diagonal, and nobody looked directly at his neighbor? For some reason none of the early park owners did this—not even Ollie Trout.)

Most of the trailers and cars are neat and trim—painted and waxed and generally well cared for. Yet the park as a whole has a dowdy look, a careless look, the look of circus grounds, the look of a camp. Neat grounds cost money, and the average trailerites aren't willing to pay a higher rent just for appearance's sake. When they gave up their ties to real estate, they unhitched their egos from the appearance of the land as well. They came to trailering from a world of well-tended lawns and freshly painted fences, and they will almost certainly return to that world before they die; but just now they're on holiday from all of that. (Ollie Trout had a full-time custodial crew to pick up trash and toys and fallen palm fronds, to prune the hibiscus bushes, to whitewash the bathrooms and manicure the grass. But then Ollie Trout was an exlandscaper and an ex-pitchman, and he wore bright blue trousers and smoked big cigars and charged every rig five to ten dollars a week for rent without batting an eye, in an era when $1.25 was considered tops. The Ollie Trout Camp, right on Biscayne Boulevard, had room for three hundred trailers, and during the winter season in Miami it was nearly always full.)

At first glance these trailerites seem to have divested themselves of so many of the trappings of middle-class ostentation—the house beautiful, the better homes and gardens—and yet just listen to their conversations: they know the name and the price tag and the reputation of every car and every trailer that pulls into the park. One might argue for hours the superiority of his $795 Vagabond over his neighbor's $850 Elcar, yet he and the neighbor are both waiting eagerly for their first look at the new, seven-and-a-half-foot-wide Gliders coming out of that big plant up in Chicago.

They boast of their frugality, but their automobiles belie them—always as shiny and new, always as loaded with extras as they can possibly afford. For all their Spartan life style, these neogypsies seem nearly as thing-conscious, as gadget-hungry, as status-sensitive as anyone else in American society. Part of them loves their primitive life style: playing house outside under the trees, feeling the stormy night winds that rock their little plywood cradles, enjoying the birdsongs and flowersmells that float through the open windows and drift across their dinner tables. But at the same time, they wouldn't mind having just a little more room, a little more gadgetry, a few more creature comforts—as soon as they can afford them.

Odd ducks, these American trailerites: people as full of contradictions as a backwoods politician. Partly from idealism, partly from economic need, and partly from sheer rebelliousness, they created an entirely new kind of community. It's a community in which individuals and their homes come and go at will, but the social structure somehow remains magically intact. It's an idyllic community, in many ways: one in which the pursuit of happiness seems really to have displaced the pursuit of status; one in which friendliness seems more important than wealth. A sheltered little world, this, free from the sins of envy, pride and gluttony—and three out of seven isn't bad—where nobody need feel any pressure to compare themselves with the Joneses.

Trailers had model-years, just like cars, and each fall the trailerites went "tire kicking," to see how much longer and wider and more luxurious the new models had grown.

Nobody? Then why is it that each year the trailers—just like the cars that pull them—keep getting bigger and fancier? Why are the '38 models so much longer and heavier than the '37s, the '39s even wider and gaudier than the '38s? And why do the trailerites respond so eagerly to the rumors of airconditioning and central heat, of second stories and tip-out bedrooms, that are spreading through the camps in '39, right along with the rumors of war in Europe? Are they really content with the simple and unpretentious life they've created? Or is it possible that, somewhere deep in their egalitarian souls, bigger is still better, newer is really nicer? Are they already beginning to chafe, beginning to outgrow their utopia even before it's fully matured? Are the seeds of its destruction located, not in the anger and prejudice of outsiders, but right in the trailerite's own inscrutable heart?

8 Go Back Where You Came From

A time limit could be fixed within which each trailer should become a dwelling, complying with front, side, and rear yard requirements, or move on. . . . Under such conditions it would not be possible for the trailer owners to stay very long in one city.
> —*Edward M. Bassett,* Planning and Civic Comment, *1937*

"Do you mean there are people who don't like trailerites?"
> —*Ruth Bowlus, widow of William Hawley Bowlus,*
> *in conversation, 1988*

Life on the parks went on. People got up in the morning, consulted their barometer, and then went off—depending on their age—to school or work or play. In the evening they came home, ate, lazed about on the patio reading or visiting, darning socks or tying flies, and then padded off to bed, consulting the barometer again on the way. Barometers were as common as canaries among the early trailerites, especially in the beach parks along the hurricane-prone Gulf Coast. Almost every trailer family owned one, and each family privately considered theirs to be the only really reliable instrument in the whole camp. A kind of household god, the family barometer shared a mirrored whatnot shelf in the living room with seashells and ceramic figurines and pictures of relatives back home. Or else it hung outside the door on a special hook, because a lot of folk just couldn't shake the idea that a barometer was bound to be more accurate out there where it could keep an eye on the weather firsthand. One of the earliest images I carry from the parks is of an old man, a bachelor neighbor, leaning out the door in

> *" 'Tis with our Judgements as our Watches, none Go just alike, yet each believes his own."*
> —Alexander Pope

pajamas and stocking nightcap, flashlight in hand, scowling up his nose at his barometer beneath a fingernail moon and a skyload of stars.

Weather was as important to the trailerites as it was to farmers, and not only because they lived so nearly outside, in huts made of canvas and veneer, but because, like farmers, they had so much at stake. A sudden windstorm in the night could destroy an awning worth two weeks' salary, set its spiked poles whipping and flailing against the trailer's leatherette skin, blow the family barometer off its hook and break it all to hell and gone. An unexpected midnight shower meant climbing out of bed to crank down the ceiling ventilators and pull all the windows in a few notches. Every stray gust of wind sent a tremor through the framework of these frail, floating bungalows, registering itself, whether the owners were asleep or awake, on the delicate seismograph of their consciousness.

CYCLONE PROVES STRUCTURAL STRENGTH OF ELCAR TRAILERS
—headline, *Trailer Topics,* July 1939

Storms and the threat of storms were much on the mind of the thirties trailerites, so they shouldn't have been caught off guard by the storm of public anger brewing outside their little park-world—the storm that had been set off by Roger Babson's thunderbolt of 1936: "Within two decades, one out of every two Americans will be living in a trailer." In less than a year the first warm gusts of public curiosity had blown themselves out, and the fickle wind of opinion began to shift. But the trailerites, despite their weather eye, either missed this change or failed to take it seriously. They shouldn't have been caught off guard when the storm began to break around them—but they were.

Prejudice—prejudgment passed on other individuals—is an ugly habit, and nobody is free of it—certainly not the trailerites themselves. Like the tin can tourists who preceded them—like most Americans today—the trailerites of the thirties inhabited a relatively narrow band within the broad spectrum of American culture.

Despite their professed ideals of equality and gregariousness, they were, as a group, far from cosmopolitan. Though most of them had come to trailering from an urban background, their roots and ideals were nevertheless rural, and relatively narrow. As they swirled and eddied about the country like fall leaves, they naturally congealed into camps of like-minded, like-cultured, like-skinned folk: lily white ghettos of midwestern working-class Protestants, for the most part. Despite

their itinerant life, they thought of themselves as belonging to the pre-
dominant—the mainstream—American culture.

As a group, they were only vaguely aware of other cultures within
the country: Jewish people, blacks, Hispanics, the urban, the poor.
These other ways of being American seldom impinged upon the trailerites' daily lives. Their next-door neighbors—the people they saw
every morning in the shaving mirror, the people they shared laundry
tub and clothesline with—were seldom urban or poor, seldom Jewish
or black or Hispanic, especially in the parks of the Deep South, where
the racial lines were drawn even more clearly than elsewhere. But wherever the trailerites went—north, south, east, or west—their neighbors
tended to be people who looked like them and cooked like them, and
this homogeneity of culture was no doubt one of the latent appeals of
trailer life during the thirties and forties—just as it is to the millions
in mobile home communities today.

To deal on a daily basis with all kinds of people—with people of
varying habits and beliefs and appearances and values—requires a fund
of psychic energy and flexibility that the trailerites were already drawing
heavily upon just by moving about as often as they did. A new job, a
new town, a new climate—these are, for the average person, more than
enough novelty to swallow in a single dose. So if the trailerites didn't
consciously seek out a safe and comfortable ghetto of their own kind,
they were nevertheless pleased when they found one—so pleased that
they immediately unhitched, rolled out their awning, hung up the
canary and went next door to glad hand the new neighbors.

Your friends are my friends and my friends are your friends. This
was not—at least not deliberately—a hypocritical ideal. But in practice,
among the trailerites as among the tin canners before them, it almost
always turned out that your friends and my friends looked and dressed
and swore and worshipped pretty much alike.

And so the trailerites, despite their self-image as citizens of the world,
quickly came to be as insular as any other group in the American
cultural matrix. And why not? Didn't everything in their little six-acre
world conspire to convince them that they resided very near to the hub
of the universe? Didn't the milkman and the iceman and the paperboy
and even the butcher bring their wares right to the door? Didn't the

"Practically every trailer
park of appreciable size
has become a community
within a community."
—*The New York Times*,
February 7, 1937

"A community in itself
with drug store, grocery,
meat market, barber
shop, community hall,
fishing, boating and
bathing."
—St. Petersburg, Florida,
park ad, *Trailer Travel*,
October 1936

park have its own grocery store and gas station, right on the boulevard out front? In many of the parks, visitors from "outside" were required to stop at the office and were announced grandly over the public address system, like guests at a ball. So, too, were the trailerites' rare phone calls: "Telephone for Buleah Morton in space twenty-seven . . . Telephone for Mrs. Morton in twenty-seven." (A call to the phone— or a telegram—would bring neighbors to their doors with concern on their faces, for in the era of twice a day mail delivery only bad news traveled by wire.)

Insular: the lily white magazines they read—*Liberty, American, Coronet, The Reader's Digest, The Saturday Evening Post*—and the lily white programs that came scratching and whistling through their little wooden radios—"Stella Dallas," "The Great Gildersleeve," "Fibber McGee and Molly"—all of these were about people who, though they might have bigger closets, seemed to be very much like themselves. Everything in their world reinforced the trailerites' sense of membership in Club America, their certainty of being among the people referred to in "We, the people. . . ."

So when they ventured out of their little self-sufficient ghettos, trailer in tow, and encountered genuine hostility, when they found themselves stereotyped and prejudged exactly like any other minority group, when they discovered that, in the eyes of much of the nation, house trailers might be cute but the people who lived in them were, *ipso facto,* undesirables, low-class, trash, they were invariably shocked.

Few writers of the period articulated this shock better than Konrad Bercovici in a two-part article published in *Harper's Monthly* in the spring of 1937. Bercovici, like most of the people who wrote about the trailer movement during the thirties, was not a full-time trailerite. He and his wife and two daughters bought a fifteen-foot Covered Wagon and towed it twice across America during the summer of '36—the summer of the first full bloom of the trailer fad. To Bercovici, trailering was a lark, not a way of life, even though his entire family fell madly in love with this pseudo-gypsy existence.

But of course the average American made no distinction between part-timers and full-timers, between homeowners on vacation and the people who had actually sold the farm and rallied to the cry of escape taxes and rent. To the average stay-at-home American, every trailer

"It was easy to ferret out the implication. People who lived in trailers were the social equivalent of carrion."
—Clinton Twiss,
The Long, Long Trailer, 1952

owner was beginning to look like one of those "gasoline gypsies," who, according to *The New York Times*, "pays less for social services than any other citizen in these tax-ridden United States." On the Bercovici's third night out, they encountered the first of these average Americans:

> I had pulled up before night had fallen (for we had vowed never to travel at night) at a cabin camp, and asked the woman who had come out whether we could spend the night there. She screamed, "I won't have any trailers on my grounds. And move on. Let's see you move on," she ordered as she showed me the way with her long finger.
>
> I didn't stop to ask the reason for her lack of hospitality.
>
> "I'll pay you," I assured her.
>
> "Get off the grounds," she yelled.
>
> We felt rather humiliated at being ordered off like tramps.

Recovering their dignity, the Bercovicis sailed southward, pondering the strange hostility of this hosteler. No doubt the first flowering of the trailer fad must have seemed a grave threat to the young and still struggling tourist cabin industry. But already the more progressive cabin owners had begun to recognize the trailer trade as an adjunct to their business, and many were already busy clearing a little land beside their court and stringing lights and power wires. Perhaps, the Bercovicis concluded, this woman's hostility had been a mere fluke.

Not so. Even down in the Sunshine State, where tourists were welcomed at county lines with complimentary road maps and free glasses of orange juice, the family fared little better:

> I have met almighty sheriffs in Florida who thought that no trailer ought to be allowed to roll upon the sacred Floridian roads, meant only for the higher class of cars. Over and over again I heard that the people traveling in trailers were not the kind that Florida wanted; that they were undesirables. Had the sheriffs and hotelkeepers manufactured the ocean and the sun they couldn't have exhibited a more proprietary attitude.

The European-born Bercovici was deeply offended by such cavalier treatment in his chosen country, the land of the free. Although discrimination is not the main thrust of his lengthy *Harper's* article, the theme recurs:

At present the local officials look upon the trailer traveler as an outcast, a man without a vote, without a home, without a fireplace, and who is only tolerated for the while, until some laws will be made that will wipe him off the face of the earth. Adverse publicity has succeeded in making people believe that the trailer traveler is living at the expense of the rest of the population; that he is a tax cheater; that his children go to school without paying taxes to the State. A grocery man in Virginia looked upon my trailer and denounced all trailer people as cheats. "You ain't paying no taxes—no taxes," he screamed, in a high piping voice. The tax on gas in Virginia is 7 cents a gallon. I pointed out to him that since almost any trailer car would use at least five gallons of gasoline a day, a man who owned a trailer paid at least 35 cents a day in taxes, to the State and the government, which was more than $100 a year, which was more than the average tax paid by the average United States citizen. But he wouldn't be enlightened. "You ain't paying no taxes. You are like gypsies. I hate gypsies."

In print at least, Bercovici seemed willing to turn the other cheek. "Such people," he concludes philosophically,

> envy the passing trailers as the worm envies the bird's ability to fly. Envy brews hatred. In Alabama they wouldn't let our trailer be parked in front of a restaurant while we were eating inside.
>
> "Eat elsewhere. We didn't send for you. Go back where you came from."

This sort of provincialism, of regional chauvinism, is far from dead in America today (although it probably hasn't been *that* healthy for years). Of course Bercovici had a couple of strikes against him before he came to bat. For starters, he was traveling through the Deep South with Connecticut license plates. And in the thirties the Deep South was a lot deeper, a lot more convoluted and Faulknerian, than it is today. My parents, on their honeymoon trip down the East Coast in '39, made lifelong friends of their landlords in Atlanta, an elderly couple named Perdue. Mr. Perdue—he was so old and so southern and so genteel that he never had a first name in our family mythology—told them repeatedly, over the years, that they were both "mighty fine, mighty fine people, fo' Yankees." My folks understood this as high praise from a man born in General Sherman's footsteps, less than five years after Appomattox.

"I don't give a damn how they do it up north."
—bumper sticker, Houston, Texas, 1980s

Secondly, Bercovici was undoubtedly handicapped by his accent. He traveled the back roads by choice, and a European-born Connecticut Yankee isn't going to disappear into the crowd in rural Alabama today, much less in the summer of '36—the summer James Agee and Walker Evans were down there researching their sharecropper book, *Let Us Now Praise Famous Men*. As a child—a trailer child—I lived all over the South during the forties, and never once encountered the kind of raw hostility Bercovici records. But a child is more flexible than an adult—especially a child whose Yankee father is fond of repeating, "When in Rome, do as the Georgians do. And the same goes for Athens and Atlanta." As a child, I never forgot where I was—always remembered to say "trailer house" in the South and Southwest, and "house trailer" elsewhere; never called a bayou a creek, or vice-versa; and kept in mind that, in Tuscaloosa, "afternoon" might mean anytime before 8:00 P.M. Easy.

I learned early—and instinctively—that "good English" and "bad English" aren't particularly useful terms in America, despite what your teacher might have told you. Better to talk about appropriate and inappropriate diction. Example: You're sitting in a bar in Houston and someone rushes in and says, "Man, you shoulda seen the wreck Ah diss seen out there—teeth, hair an' eye-balls flyin' everwhir!" If you reply, "Oh, I should like to have seen that!" you may be using perfectly good English, but you're going to shut that bar down quicker than Carrie Nation. The correct response, the appropriate diction (unless you're simply determined to stop the whole scene, focus all the energy on yourself, and maybe catch an early flight out the front door) is to answer, "N-o-o shee-yit?"

Judging by the hostility he encountered, Bercovici must have made little attempt to downplay his alienness, to pick up the local diction, to blend in with his surroundings as he traveled. It wouldn't have been easy, of course, for he and his family were trailer travelers, not trailer dwellers. In their three-month tour they were seldom unhitched— seldom disassociated from that "strange whale behind a fish-shaped car" that marked them as trailerites. And as the thirties wore on, more and more people became hostile toward trailerites.

"I do not understand why there should be so much talk against

> "I got called a damn Yankee and a furriner and ordered out of the house or off the premises more times than I have hairs on my head. I'll tell you, those Texans are rough on Northerners."
> —1930s Fuller Brush salesman interviewed by John Deck in *Rancho Paradise*, 1972

> "Where rolling homes have been deemed liabilities either socially or commercially, they are treated as beggars might be, given an hour to get out of town."
> —*Sociology & Social Research*, July–August 1938

trailers," a young father says in one of Cowgill's 1938 case studies of trailer life, "if America wants trailers they should have them."

But America, except for a few hundred thousand victims of trailer fever, did not want trailers—at least not in the quantities that began pouring forth from magazine and newspaper stories during the hoopla period of 1936 and early 1937:

> According to the most conservative trailer men, there will be a U.S. market of at least 400,000 units a year by 1940 (*Time,* June 15, 1936).

> 1,000,000 people will be living in trailers by the end of this month, estimates the American Automobile Association (*The Architectural Record,* December 1936).

> This year's production is calculated at a possible 400,000 units by some 400 manufacturers (*Literary Digest,* May 15, 1937).

> Two million people will be trailing through the country in a year from now, and five million in five years (Bercovici in *Harper's,* May 1937).

Ten thousand new trailers a month. Two hundred thousand—no, make that four hundred thousand—a year! Of course no such quantities ever poured out of the trailer factories themselves. All these figures, and a hundred more like them, were pure fabrications, speculations—lies—made up by journalists hungry for a story and by a few of the trailermen who were anxious to hang onto their new-found national importance. In 1936 and early '37 it was far easier to manufacture lies than house trailers, and the market for both seemed to be insatiable.

The true factory output figures for the period were somewhat less impressive: the top fifty or sixty manufacturers turned out something like fifty-five thousand trailers in 1937. At least half that many more flowed from back yard builders and the smaller firms, for a total of around ninety thousand units—a far cry from the 200 to 400 thousand the headlines had predicted. Withal, 1937 was the biggest production year of the prewar decade, up almost twenty thousand units from the first boom year, 1936.

Partly because of the thousands of home-builts, and partly because so many of the smaller factories went unreported, accurate figures on the total number of trailers on the road in these years were simply

During the twenties and thirties, thousands of people designed and built their own trailers. This Ohio model, photographed in Washington, D.C., in 1941, sports a clerestory roof and dropped entryway.

impossible to attain. In the mid-thirties, not every state required an automobile trailer—or even a truck trailer—to be licensed, which isn't surprising: in 1937, with everybody driving huge, cow-hipped automobiles capable of over 100 mph, five states—Florida, Illinois, Louisiana, Mississippi and South Dakota—still hadn't gotten around to licensing their drivers, and a dozen others issued an operator's license to anybody who walked in the door with the required fee—no written test, no driving test, no questions asked. (A junior senator from Missouri named Harry S. Truman was already busy introducing federal legislation to override this regional insanity.) To add to the confusion, those states that did issue trailer licenses seldom distinguished between passenger car trailers and truck trailers—and long-distance trucking was another mushrooming industry during the Depression.

Only one state, Virginia, kept separate records on house trailers at this time, and in the spring of 1937 its motor vehicle department released a set of figures that surprised even the most optimistic of trailermen, a set of figures that made Roger Babson's prediction of "half of America" moving into house trailers seem almost conservative:

> In the eight months from March 1 to November 1, 1936, the state of Virginia licensed 5,678 housetrailers, more than twelve times as many as were licensed during 1926 and twice as many as in 1935 (*The American City,* March 1937).

What? House trailer registrations doubling, maybe even tripling, in a single year? The timing of this announcement could hardly have been worse, for this lone statistic—correct, but, as it turned out, wildly aberrant—precipitated a whole summer of fearmongering headlines: THREE MILLION TRAILERITES BY YEAR'S END . . . TRAILER INVASION WORRIES CAPE COD . . . FLORIDA CITIES BAN TRAILERS . . . 50,000 TRAILER CHILDREN SWAMP CALIFORNIA SCHOOLS. . . .

Many of the smaller trailer builders were delighted by the Virginia announcement—particularly when it brought flocks of wide-eyed journalists running to them for corroboration. A number of them responded by puffing up their chests and delivering yet another round of absurdly overblown predictions: sales projections some five to ten times beyond their actual output capabilities were not uncommon. Big figures, the trailermen reasoned, make big headlines; and who knows—saying it just might make it come true.

But the effect on the public of all this hyperbole was not exactly what the builders intended. Instead of fueling the fad, it fueled the fire. The idea of three million Americans living on wheels by the end of 1937 may have rung sweetly upon the trailerman's ear, but it just plain frightened average citizens—not to mention their city councils and state senators. And the first tendency of frightened people is to fight back—sometimes even before they're hurt.

America's towns and cities began to react. The tiny village of Orchard Lake, northwest of Detroit, had already achieved the honor of being first in the nation to ban the house trailer, had already set a precedent, by late 1936, for the growing antitrailer sentiment in the country. Both *Time* and *Newsweek* covered the story; and United Press wired blow-by-blow details of the case to half the newspapers in the United States.

Back in the spring of '35, it seems, one Hildred Gumarsol, a factory worker in nearby Pontiac, had bought himself a small trailer and towed it down to Orchard Lake, parking it in a lot behind his bachelor brother's house. There he promptly set it up on sawhorses, pulled off its wheels, and tacked together a screened-in porch to keep the Michigan mosquitoes at bay. Then he lit up a Lucky and settled down with the missus for a carefree summer at the lake.

The idea of trailer-as-lakeside-cabin seemed like a good one, and in due time the Gumarsols were joined by four or five other rigs, each of them slipping Hildred's brother a twenty for the season's rent, which included all the well water you could carry, plus free and unrestricted use of the Gumarsol family outhouse. At this point, some of the neighbors began to grumble. These trailer people, these out-of-towners, were using the lake, and the streets of Orchard Lake Village, and its police and fire protection, without paying a plug nickel's worth of property tax. And some of the trailerites, according to rumor, weren't any too careful about where they changed into their bathing suits, either. A class issue was developing here, with the people in clapboard houses looking squarely down their noses at the people in masonite. That summer, in Orchard Lake, the word "trash" was heard more often than "garbage."

Come fall, the other trailers hitched up and drifted south, but Hildred and his wife simply boarded up their rig and drove home to Pontiac without it. When this same little circus came back for a return engagement the following summer, the neighbors decided they'd had enough: early in August they appealed to the law. Hildred Gumarsol, they averred, was using his trailer as a house, and a village ordinance required a house to be a minimum of four hundred square feet.

"Nonsense," Gumarsol replied via his lawyer, "a trailer isn't a house—it's a vehicle. It has a vehicle license plate, see?"

Arthur Green, the local JP, who described himself to a *Newsweek* reporter as "just a common, ordinary hayseed justice of the peace," recognized the Orchard Lake case as a landmark, and took his sweet time deliberating it. August drifted by, then September. Gumarsol and the missus returned once more to Pontiac; their fellow trailerites again dispersed. Along toward the middle of cool, windy November, Justice Green finally delivered his verdict:

It is the opinion of this court that a house trailer of the type occupied by the defendant and having a great many of the appointments of a modern home would come under the scope of a human dwelling whether it stands upon blocks or the wheels attached thereto or whether it be coupled to or detached from an automobile.

The law had spoken. Gumarsol's little trailer was a house, not a vehicle, and Hildred Gumarsol was therefore guilty of violating the village housing ordinance. Since it was a test case, and since Justice Green had never before made the pages of *Time* and *Newsweek,* the good JP fined the defendant—in absentia—a dollar and costs, $4.10 total, tossing in, at no extra charge, this rumination:

The advent of the house trailer is revolutionizing social conditions. . . . A portion of the American people are bound to become nomadic. In this event it is fitting that municipalities prepare to meet these condi-tions. Those that court the tourist trade should make proper provisions therefor. Those that do not should, like Orchard Lake Village, pass ordinances so drastic that it would be unprofitable to obtain a license to permit the parking of house trailers.

"Ordinances so drastic. . . ." Hayseed JP or no, that sounded like sweet good sense to the city of Palm Beach, down in trailer-ridden Florida. The Palm Beach city council promptly passed just such a dras-tic ordinance, permitting these wandering homes a maximum of sixty minutes stay within the city limits—provided no cooking was done during that hour. Miami Beach and Grand Rapids read the Palm Beach law and found it unnecessarily verbose: they simplified theirs to no trailers, period. So did Atlantic City and Lincoln, Nebraska, followed, on the West Coast, by Palo Alto and Eugene.

Other towns opted for subtler forms of legislation, which soon came to be known within the trailerite grapevine as "scram laws." Peoria Heights, Illinois, levied a fifty-dollar-per-year tax on its trailers, but since the going rate was three to five dollars, nobody stayed in town to pay such a fee, which was exactly what Peoria Heights had in mind. Rochester, New York, required its trailer owners to buy a special permit, revocable at any time, in order to live in their wheeled homes, while up in the Pacific Northwest, Seattle opened its cool and cloudy heart to any trailer that came along, provided only that it contained a bath, a sink, and a toilet—in other words, any trailer that cost $1,500 and upwards, any trailer belonging to the filthy and unabashedly rich.

Such total exclusion policies almost immediately proved to be short-sighted. Banned from town, most of the trailers simply scuttled out to the city limits and dropped anchor again, right on the municipal door-step but just beyond its jurisdiction. The trailer problem simply refused to go away. Like a mosquito brushed at halfheartedly, it moved slightly out of reach and then settled down again, more determined than ever.

In the muddled minds of city fathers from Hyannisport to San Diego, it slowly became obvious that the automobile trailer was not just an-other passing fad, like pedal cars and marathon dancing; it was here to stay. A certain minority of Americans, it seemed, were determined to make their homes in these fragile and often unlovely little contrap-tions, the law and public opinion be damned. Sooner or later the entire question of how to regulate and tax the house trailer was going to require that bane of bureaucricies, that gorgon of governments: new thinking.

The city of Detroit—Arthur Sherman's hometown, birthplace of the trailer industry, home to a dozen or more fledgling trailer manufactur-ing plants—was typical of many U.S. cities in its handling of the trailer problem. As early as 1920, Detroit already harbored a colony of full-time trailer dwellers within its city limits: eight or ten families of poorly paid industrial workers clustered on a suburban lot in crude homemade wagons, most without satisfactory water supply and waste plumbing, most with only the barest form of heating and insulation. This first Detroit trailer camp was, by any standards, little more than a slum on wheels—in a city that had its share of slums on foundations.

No one paid much attention to these primitive trailer dwellers—they were so few in number, and so tenuous, paying their parking fees by the week, always apparently just on the verge of rolling, or starving, or blowing, away. Not bad people, you understand. Not bad neighbors, even. Just desperately, conspicuously poor. A little more industrious, a little less triflin' (my father's Ohio farm boy term for lazy) than your auto-tramps and wagon tramps—those people with similar rigs who roamed the highways. These folk stayed put at least—stayed put, held down jobs, and managed as best they could. At the time, most of the

"If enough people in To-ledo wanted to live in trees the city would have to make some provision [for them] to do so."
—statement by Toledo city councilman during trailer ordinance debate, 1938

neighbors seemed to agree that this first Detroit trailer camp was, to quote one of them, "no trouble at all."

But with the Depression the trailerites' numbers grew. By 1930 there were four such camps within the Detroit city limits; by 1935, nine. More and more people, it seemed, were beginning to discover the virtues of trailer life. And not just the poor, but retirees as well, and an increasing number of the great, sprawling, blue-collar working class. More people in more trailers, needing more parking spaces, more water and schools and sewers and hospitals and garbage pick-up.

At this point, Detroit property owners, like those in Orchard Lake, began to grumble, first to the newspapers, then to the health authorities, then to the truant officers and the police, and finally to the common council. Property taxes, the grumblers acknowledged, can never be entirely fair, but these trailer people weren't paying any property taxes at all. Even a slum apartment building put *something* back in the tax coffers. Detroit's trailer camps were still on the rolls as undeveloped property. What did the common council plan to do about this inequity?

The council's first response was quick and candid: we'll throw 'em out, they said. We'll sic the board of health on these trailer people and force them to cease and desist their slumming.

A decade earlier, back in the days of Calvin Coolidge and bathtub gin, such an approach might have gone unchallenged. But Coolidge was dead, and his prosperity as well. By 1936, social arrogance, like bobbed hair, had gone out of style in America. A new age had dawned: the age of Franklin Roosevelt and the New Deal, the age of the common man, the age of the underdog. Immediately, a couple of Detroit labor unions jumped to the trailerites' defense. So did a local civil rights group, and a newly formed trailerite organization called The Mobile Home Owners' Association of America.

But the common council's biggest stumbling block turned out to be a handful of trailer builders who had banned together tentatively in the summer of '36 as the Trailer Coach Manufacturers' Association. The TCMA was small, even though it included all of the biggest names in the midwestern trailer game: Covered Wagon, Silver Dome, Kozy-Coach, Vagabond, Schult, Alma, Palace, Travelo, U.S. Coach. Because the organization was new and dues were strictly voluntary, the TCMA didn't have a lot of money. But it had an axe to grind—mistreatment

"From Detroit comes news of a trailer city designed for year-round use by tenants permanently employed in the motor capital."
—*Architectural Record*, December 1936

of its customers—and in the spring of '37 it inherited, fresh from the Pontiac division of General Motors, a man named James L. Brown.

Brown was not one of the trailer industry's founding fathers. He didn't get his start by hammering together two-wheel campers in his back yard, the way most trailermen had. Jim Brown was a former car dealer with a law degree from George Washington University. He was also a CPA. He had over nine years of marketing experience with GM when Arthur Sherman hired him to help sell Covered Wagons. Brown was the author of three books on sales management. He was bright and articulate, and he had a way of looking at today and seeing tomorrow in it. In an industry composed overwhelmingly of amateurs, Jim Brown was a pro.

As a newcomer, the first thing Brown noticed about this little group of trailer builders was how all of them kept lying to themselves, and to each other, and to the press, about their product. They were advertising and promoting travel trailers, but they were selling house trailers, mobile homes, because that's what people wanted and needed and could afford in the middle of the Great Depression. Brown wasn't shy about pointing this out, although no one in the industry particularly wanted to hear it.

The next thing Brown noticed was that the customers, the people who were buying all these travel trailers, were starting to get the bum's rush in towns and cities all over America. Far too often they were being treated as undesirables, deprived of what lawyer Brown saw as their constitutional right to the reasonable use of their new home—er, trailer coaches. This the manufacturers seemed willing to hear. You bet, they said; bum's rush; unconstitutional. Why don't you speak up for 'em, Jim? Starting right here in Detroit.

So Jim Brown did. He joined the trailerites' lawyer Benjamin Robinson in presenting the case for mobile living to the Detroit Common Council. Property owners, Brown argued, have certain rights which must be respected, and so do trailer owners, because trailers are property, too. So here's our proposal for satisfying the needs of both groups: Let the city set aside land for a municipal trailer park, to be run in an orderly and sanitary fashion at a small profit, and let Detroit's trailer dwellers move there, and stay as long as they like. That's how they do it down in Florida, and it works well.

The council's first response, fueled by the ire of realtors and apartment owners and knots of angry neighbors, sounded something like this: we don't give a damn how they do it down south. What the council gave, instead, was the nod to the board of health, and the board of health promptly began handing out trailer eviction notices all over town, for by now the Detroit trailer population was scattered among a dozen or more camps in every quadrant of the city.

Jim Brown understood that politics is the art of compromise, and that law is merely a specialized form of politics. While lawyer Robinson took the board of health to court and got a temporary stay on the eviction notices, lawyer Brown hammered away at the council, giving and taking, proposing and counterproposing, always quietly and reasonably, always with his eye on the big picture, because that was his style.

But Brown's position was not a comfortable one, for almost alone among TCMA members, he was quite certain that the future of the trailer industry lay in housing, not camping. He knew that Justice Green, the hayseed JP from Orchard Lake, was dead right—trailers were dwellings, not vehicles—and that until the automobile trailer was recognized in every municipality in America as an acceptable form of year-round habitation, it wasn't going anywhere. But this was the summer of 1937; the trailer industry was still booming along mindlessly, riding the crest of a wave it didn't pretend to understand, and Brown hardly dared express this opinion among his fellow manufacturers, much less before the common council of Detroit.

So when the Detroit trailer ordinance was finally passed in July, most of the manufacturers and trailerites saw it as a victory. But Jim Brown felt largely defeated. Although not a single one of Detroit's 250 or more "full-timers" had been forced to leave town, and although a reasonable set of standards for parks—private, not municipal—had been agreed upon, the antitrailer forces in the council had managed to slap a ninety-day-per-year time limit on a trailer's stay in Motor City.

Three months and you're out.

Oakland, California, had done the same thing the previous September; but Oakland was not the cradle of the house trailer industry; Detroit was. And if Detroit wouldn't take the trailer seriously—

By 1935, trailers had evolved from crude camping devices into viable homes, and thousands of American families had begun living in them all year round.

wouldn't recognize it as anything more substantial than a plaything, a summer vacation toy—then who would?

Jim Brown was in a frustrating position. All around him were people with their heads buried in the sand. The manufacturers were still trying to pretend that the trailers they were building were destined to become baubles for the rich, that their primary customers were mansioned movie stars and Fortune 500 industrialists—people who could afford to invest upwards of eight hundred Depression dollars in a vacation vehicle, a mere gadget. And the legislators—city and county and state—were still acting as if the trailer were just another bothersome fad that could be discouraged, sent elsewhere, by passing a few laws:

"It cannot be said in all honesty that the extremely affluent were among our first customers."
—Airfloat founder Omar Suttles, 1976

"Those that court the tourist trade should make proper provisions therefor. Those that do not should, like Orchard Lake Village, pass ordinances so drastic. . . ."

No one seemed willing, in the summer of 1937, to face the simple fact that the American house trailer had outgrown its camper stage, its toy stage, sometime back about 1935. It had already become a viable alternative home, and it wasn't going to go away. No one was yet willing to acknowledge that ways were going to have to be found to tax these new American citizens, the trailerites, so that they might carry their fair share of the cost of schools and libraries and sidewalks and streets and policemen and water systems and sewage plants, whether they chose to stay in town for a week or a decade. Ways were going to have to be found to regulate their parking, without unduly curtailing their liberty, so that this new and lighthearted life style wouldn't threaten the property values of homeowners nearby.

All this seemed obvious to lawyer Brown, but Brown was not your average American. To the average citizens, and their councils, this trailer foolishness had gone just about far enough. A year and a half of hullabaloo had only left them confused. Weren't these trailer things supposed to be for vacations, like the ads said? Then what was all this talk about people living in them year-round?

"One thing's for certain: nobody's neighborhood needs a lot of strangers moving in—a lot of out-of-staters. Especially if they're going to live like circus people and gypsies. That might be OK down in Florida—they say everybody's from out of state, down there—but we're not having any of it here, thank you.

"What we need are a few stiff laws—something to keep these bums from swarming in here and taking our jobs and putting their disease-ridden kids into our schools. What's wrong with their own town, anyway, that they got to come here and ruin ours? We didn't send for 'em. Let 'em go back where they came from."

"The trailer owner is really a smart man; he is pioneering a new way of living."
—James L. Brown, *Trailer Topics,* Spring 1938

9 All Good Things

We find that whole communities suddenly fix their minds upon one object, and go mad in its pursuit; that millions of people become simultaneously impressed with one delusion, and run after it, till their attention is caught by some new folly more captivating than the first.

—*Charles Mackay,* Extraordinary Popular Delusions and the Madness of Crowds, *1852*

Despite the gathering storm, despite the rumblings in city councils and state legislatures across the land, despite even the growing animosity of the editorial writers, those bellwethers of the national herd, America's trailer manufacturers sailed into 1937 under full canvas. As well they might. The economic signs, on the surface, at least, were rosy. As the year began, even the most conservative trailermen looked forward to a doubling, maybe even a tripling of their 1936 business—and 1936 had been, by almost any measure, the Year of the Trailer. Nothing since Lindbergh's flight to Paris had so captured the public imagination as the house trailer did during the summer and fall of 1936.

Almost overnight, it seemed, trailers and trailer life had become the familiar fare of theater newsreels, newspaper feature stories and editorial pages, radio "soaps," comic strips (Ella Cinders bought an Indian), and popular fiction. Out in Hollywood, Sam Goldwyn hired Barbara Stanwyck and Joel McCrea and began assembling a supporting cast for the first trailer movie, to be called *Heaven on Wheels,* while press agents ground out reams of trailer-related gossip: Gypsy Rose Lee "just loved" her new Covered Wagon, and W. C. Fields had ordered his latest trailer equipped with a modern Dictaphone and—naturally—a wet bar. *The Chicago Tribune* rushed into syndication a series of lightly satirical cartoons called "Trailer Tintypes" that were immediately picked up by papers all over the country. Montgomery Ward announced its

> "Wally Beery, the famous movie star, has just presented himself with a new all-metal land trailer. He plans to use the trailer on his many hunting and fishing trips."
> —M.G.M. press release, 1936

intention of adding a furnished house trailer to its catalog line, while Oxydol promised a fully equipped, nineteen-foot Covered Wagon and a brand-new Ford V-8 to each of the twenty-five winners of its grand prize sweepstakes. As the tide of trailer mania rose, every automobile dealer from Maine to California began scrambling for a trailer franchise, *any* trailer franchise, not so much for the money to be made in sales, but because the trade journals were whispering that a coach in the showroom was a sure way to double your foot traffic.

At carnivals and fairs, at supermarket openings and political rallies, wherever the ballyhoo was thickest, there someone was sure to be buying or selling or demonstrating a house trailer. With the presidential elections coming up in November, the Democrats equipped fifty snow white Hayes Coaches with loudspeakers and huge boxes of Roosevelt-Garner buttons, hitched them to fifty sleek new family sedans and sent them across the country as the "Roosevelt Caravan," a parade of prosperity as long as a freight train and twice as noisy, bringing campaign music and a tantalizing glimpse of the future to small town, working-class America.

The manufacturers themselves could claim little credit for this nationwide insanity. It was a publicity blitz beyond even Madison Avenue's abilities, and it was almost purely spontaneous—an outgrowth of the American public's seemingly endless fascination with the trailer and its possibilities. No one was more surprised, more unprepared for the hullabaloo, than the handful of builders who had risen so dramatically to the top of this sky-rocketing new industry.

To their credit, the biggest of these builders—Arthur Sherman of Covered Wagon, Norm Wolfe of Silver Dome, Dave Aerhart of Palace—continually tried to interject a voice of reason into the growing madness. At his Waldorf-Astoria press conference in November of 1936, Sherman made the point over and over that it was sociologists and journalists, not the trailer manufacturers themselves, who were predicting the "nation of nomads," the "mass exodus from the American home," and added that he never expected to see the day that trailer output would reach 400,000 a year. But such pronouncements were too sober, too pedestrian to make good headlines. People much preferred the ballyhoo.

And so, all through the second half of 1936 and into the spring and

"PAIR WED ATOP HOUSE TRAILER: With the top of a house trailer as a setting, an Elkhart couple was married Saturday night at the Michigan State Fair before a crowd of more than 3,000 persons."
—*Trailer Topics,*
September 1936

"[Sherman] himself has the air of a man startled by an avalanche brought down by an innocent step."
—*Fortune,* March 1937

summer of '37, the great, frail bubble of the trailer boom continued to swell. The house trailer revolution became, on paper at least, an accepted fact: America was headed for a nomadic lifestyle, with a large proportion of its population destined to live in gigantic trailer villages like the ones already springing up all over Florida and southern California. "Michigan trust companies are booming," *The New York Times* assured its readers in November, "as people sell their houses and their furniture, put their money in trust and take to their wheels." The American Automobile Association confidently predicted a million trailerites by the end of 1936, five million by 1940.

No one was more completely taken in by this ballyhoo than the burgeoning army of trailer retailers. Their ranks were growing daily, as hordes of out-of-work salesmen rushed to get in on this latest money-making gimmick, the trailer; in the sales parlance of the day, it was clearly a "natural." And all it took to become a trailerman was a phone number and a business card. By year's end, Covered Wagon alone had signed on nearly a thousand new dealers.

The problem was, by midsummer of '36 even the legitimate, well-established trailer dealers were months backordered; this army of anxious neophytes couldn't get their hands on so much as a display model, a sample, even by offering to pay retail! In this situation the only sensible thing for a would-be dealer to do—and this seemed to occur independently to almost every one of them—was to double, triple, maybe quadruple their backorders. So they did. And the manufacturers, seeing all these new orders roll in, reached for the phone to double their parts orders, then called in bankers and realtors and architects to talk about doubling their factory space.

The trailer industry was young and wide-eyed and inexperienced, and at this point very few actual dollars were changing hands. The dealers weren't taking deposits from the customers, and most of the manufacturers weren't taking deposits from the dealers. The entire industry, from top to bottom, was operating almost totally on faith, the business term for which is "credit." Though much smaller in scale, the situation was not unlike the long frenzy of margin-buying that had overinflated the stock market during 1928 and 1929. Certainly the driving myth was the same: nobody's got much ready cash today, but tomorrow we'll all be rich.

"Question: Would you like to own a trailer and spend part of the year traveling in it?

Answer: Yes 49.3% No 46.3% Don't know 4.4%"
—survey, *Fortune*, 1936

"The fact that they [the trailer manufacturers] have in common is that none of them has yet made much money."
—*Fortune*, March 1937

When enough people go out on the same limb together, it isn't so much a question of individuals falling off. Sooner or later the limb itself will break.

And yet, nothing ventured, nothing gained. Just four days into 1937, that most conservative of midwestern businessmen, Arthur George Sherman, bacteriologist, took the trailer industry's first, tentative step toward empire: he went public with thirty thousand shares of Covered Wagon preferred, par value twenty-five dollars. Sherman's little garage business, into which he had thus far dumped only about twelve thousand dollars of his own money, was now employing 1,100 people in a sprawling, 150,000-square-foot former refrigerator factory up in the village of Mount Clemens, a few miles above Detroit—a factory that was turning out over a thousand trailers a month and anticipating a gross sales, in 1937, of something on the order of ten million dollars.

This phenomenal success story won for Covered Wagon a publicity coup that money alone could never have bought: three full pages in Henry Luce's bright new photojournalism magazine, *Life*. Three sprawling, quarto pages of absolutely priceless fluff: absurd shots of Gatsbylike parties in trailer living rooms, the women in dark, slinky gowns, the tuxedoed men posing stiffly near the davenport (somebody's bed, by night) with their slim white fingers holding slim white cigarettes at jaunty angles to the horizontal. Pictures of trailers rolling down long assembly lines, trailers rolling down the open road, trailers perched high atop scenic mountains. And family pictures, too—a whole series of artfully staged snapshots of Mr. and Mrs. Sherman and the kids wrestling with their first tent trailer, sans wind, sans rain—pictures supposedly taken back in '28, before the Covered Wagon Company was even a gleam in Sherman's eye.

Absolutely priceless fluff, and just the thing for selling stock, and magazines, and house trailers. The *Life* pictorial hit the newsstands on February 1, a bit early, perhaps, for spring sales in the North and East, but almost perfectly timed for the big TCT winter convention down in Sarasota.

Winter convention! No matter how busy, how backordered a manufacturer might be, he couldn't afford to miss the winter convention. The advice the old man in red suspenders had given Arthur Sherman at the Detroit auto show back in 1930 was probably the only good advice Sherman ever got about the trailer business: "You wanna sell these things, forget about auto shows. You wanna sell these things, join the Tin Can Tourists. Git yerself down to convention."

Winter convention! Every year it got bigger and better. In 1935, over a thousand rigs had shown up at Sarasota's municipal trailer park, the official TCT campsite. In '36—despite a schism among the canners and the formation of a rival group that christened itself the Automobile Tourists Association and immediately set about pirating every last by-law of the TCT, right down to its golden rule motto—the number of rigs at Sarasota topped 1,500. Over two thousand were expected in 1937. That meant six thousand potential customers—six thousand gossipy, clannish, trailer-wise old tin canners from every state in the union plus Canada, coming to gawk and kick tires and carry the word about the new models all up and down the continent. As a manufacturer, you simply had to go to Sarasota.

Not that it was such tough duty, escaping the snowbound North in February to dole out brochures and answer questions from a shaded lawn chair down on Florida's sunny west coast. The TCT usually managed to borrow a Ringling Brothers big top—the prototype of all trailer awnings, fit to cover fifty trailers—and set it up over the entire manufacturers' area, in case of rain. All you had to do was roll in beneath it with your show model, pick a spot among your competitors, unhitch, hang out the company logo, wipe a few bugs off the leatherette, and settle back for ten days of Gulf breezes and admiring crowds.

But nature, in the spring of 1937, had other plans. Late in January the weather, from the Great Lakes all the way to the Atlantic, turned unseasonably warm. Everywhere the snow melted, and the rivers began to rise. Joe Flora, business manager for Trotwood Trailers, Ohio's biggest builder, was planning to tow their newest show model down to Sarasota. He and his wife eyed the swelling streams around Trotwood and nearby Dayton, and decided to leave a few days early; they'd seen floods on the Ohio-Mississippi system before. Even so, the Floras' timing was close: trailer in tow, they slipped across the river at Cincinnati just before the state police closed the bridges.

Fighting rain and wind and detours all through the mountains of Kentucky and Tennessee, the Floras finally emerged into sunshine far down in the red earth country below Atlanta, and Trotwood was duly

In September, 1937, Covered Wagon unveiled its "Residential Model," the prototype of the 1960s mobile home. It failed disastrously; even people who loved trailers hated its square, functional ugliness. (Photo courtesy the National Automotive History Collection, Detroit Public Library.)

represented that year at winter convention. But many of the other midwestern trailer builders—and hundreds of the tin canners themselves—were turned back by the weather, and the '37 trailer show at Sarasota, normally the country's biggest, was something of a bust. It was not a good omen for the new year.

To make matters worse, the small quorum of canners at the winter convention made a disastrous decision: they voted to move their upcoming summer reunion from Sandusky, where six hundred rigs had been showing up every August, to the Menominee Indian reservation, far up in northern Wisconsin. Almost nobody came, either to the reunion or to the expensive trailer and equipment show that accompanied it. ("Just how it was expected to sell trailers to the Indians two hundred miles from nowhere is yet to be explained," *Trailer Topics* grumbled.)

Meanwhile, those upstarts, those mutineers who were calling themselves the Automobile Tourists, held their summer get-together—during the same two August weeks, naturally—at the popular Orchard Beach State Park, near Manistee, Michigan. And the ATA's gathering was, according to their suspiciously exuberant reports, a huge success. Even the accompanying trailer show was reasonably well attended, as summer shows went. Almost no dealer orders were placed, though—another bad omen. But the trailer magazine write-ups skipped lightly over this fact, and instead whooped it up over the number of manufacturers who turned out to support the new club's first summer show.

Covered Wagon was there, parading its new factory team that included not only the gadfly James Brown, lately of General Motors, but a bevy of ad managers and export experts and sales personnel plundered from the ailing auto industry—a team of marketing and production personnel befitting the world's largest manufacturer of trailer coaches. Sherman had sent a couple of show models across the lake to the ill-fated TCT exhibit at Menominee, too, but it was for the trailer show at Orchard Beach that he went all-out. It was at Orchard Beach, in August of '37, that Arthur Sherman unveiled his pride and joy, a new trailer design that was destined to be the biggest single mistake in Covered Wagon's eight-year history.

He called it their "Residential Model" and claimed it wasn't really a trailer at all, but a prefabricated house on wheels, meant to be towed from place to place "at speeds up to 25 mph." It was a full eight feet wide—the first commercially-built coach to take advantage of all the width the law allowed. Up front was a huge (by trailer standards) eight-by-ten living room; then a kitchen; then a full bath, complete with tub and shower, followed by a small bedroom in the rear. Twenty feet, overall. Fully insulated for year-round use; and fitted, as the brochures pointed out, for "easy hookup to city water and sewer." The Covered Wagon Residential: America's prototype mobile home. Inside, it was a spacious, square-cornered, cleverly designed little rolling apartment. Inside, it was somewhere between five and twenty-five years ahead of its time.

But outside, oh, outside—it was uglier than the north end of a southbound pig!

"What are you doing, Arthur Sherman? Don't you know this is 1937? Nobody wants a two-wheeled boxcar that won't do sixty on the highway—a trailer so hideously square and primitive looking that people can't believe it's not homemade. Who would have it in their park? Who would hook their sleek new Chevy to it? Who would want to be seen with such a monster? It may well be true, what Mencken said about nobody ever going broke underestimating the taste of the American public. But trailerites, Mr. Sherman, aren't your typical American public. They have their pride. They have their standards. What's more, they have their Dream.

"Oh, you've really done it this time, Father of the Industry: you've gone and insulted every last trailer addict in America—past, present and future. An entire subculture. An entire market."

To the practical but unimaginative Sherman, the "Residential" made perfect sense: if people really wanted low-cost housing, then why not give them the maximum house for their dollar? Forget streamlining; make it square and chicken coop simple, just like any other cheap shelter. Don't worry about roadability, design it for living, not for traveling. Put everything into it that people need: showers and toilets and sinks and lavatories and storage galore. Put everything into it—except the dream. Leave out the romantic, the futuristic, leave out those long, forward-sloping lines, those light, sweeping Bauhaus curves that whispered "modern" to a whole generation. Leave out that streamlined promise of speed, of flight, of escape from the mundane. Leave out all the foolishness, and put in just the necessities.

And then see how many you sell.

"Covered Wagon got the idea," *Business Week* hastily explained, "partly from the fact that a considerable percentage of coach trailers sold this year are being used for homes instead of for traveling purposes."

"Oho! So the truth comes out at last, Mr. Sherman: people are living in your Covered Wagons full-time. Back in March, according to *Fortune,* you were mostly trying to sell vacations; now you're suddenly in the housing business. Maybe you need to get your story straight, Father of the Industry. And meanwhile, you can keep your ugly $750 'Residential Model.' We'll just mosey over and take a look at those cute little streamlined Palaces, made up in Flint. They don't really look like a palace, of course—we're not that easily fooled—but at least they curve and swoop a bit. At least they look like tomorrow, not yesterday. They look *modern*. Or maybe we'll drop by the Schult display, or go see those sleek new Indians, built out in Chicago. . . ."

How quickly we discard our heroes, forgetting how rarely they come along. Palace and Schult and Indian and a hundred other brands had become overnight successes mainly by imitating Arthur Sherman's bread-loaf-style Covered Wagons, model for model, shape for shape, amenity for amenity. And now, simply by sticking to these established patterns, they had suddenly begun to narrow CW's lead in sales, to nip at the heels of the industry's only leader.

So often the key to the future lies in knowing exactly when to recycle the past. Sherman's Residential Model was roundly condemned, in 1937, for its awkward, circus wagon width, yet by 1940, every major builder was pushing out toward the eight-foot limit, and you could hardly give away those "antiquated" six-wides from the middle years of the decade. It was condemned, too, for its boxcar ugliness, and yet by the mid-fifties the mobile home industry had embraced the boxcar utterly—locked it in a death-grip from which it has yet to escape. But in the late summer of '37, the Residential's square corners struck just about everyone as being offensively old-fashioned, unutterably passé. Covered Wagon lost face, among trailermen and customers alike, over the Residential. They had stepped so far into the future that it looked like the past.

From a business point of view, it was a case of having gone out, alone, on a small branch of that tenuous limb the entire industry was clinging to. Immediately it became obvious to Sherman that nobody was going to follow, and he beat a hasty retreat, pulling the Residential out of production even before its picture appeared on the cover of *Trailer Topics*. What the father of the industry might have tried next is anybody's guess, because, late in September, his thoughts were interrupted by the snapping of a giant limb, and the American house trailer industry, Covered Wagon and all, came crashing to the ground.

Scapegoating is a natural response to misfortune. By the end of

October, every trailerman in America could tell you exactly why the industry was in a shambles—why dealers by the hundreds, many of whom had yet to get their first trailer, suddenly began canceling most, and then all, of their backorders, began declaring bankruptcy, began running off to Mexico with their unpaid-for stock; why manufacturers went to bed one night three months behind schedule and woke up the next morning three months ahead; why overstocked distributors, in a panic, started undercutting their dealers by selling direct to customers, while the manufacturers above them did exactly the same. Every trail-erman, from company president to the lowest salesman, knew exactly why the bough had broken—and of course it had nothing to do with themselves.

The culprit, most of them agreed, was a fellow named Clarence Buddington Kelland. Kelland, a popular author of fiction, had pub-lished, back in May, a long, rambling piece of antitrailer satire called "How's Your Hitch?" The piece appeared in *The Saturday Evening Post*, America's blue-collar bible, and it focused on three main points—the scarcity of good parks, the shoddy engineering of a particular trailer that Kelland had bought, and the industry's woeful lack of standard-ization, especially in the area of hitches:

> The hitch is the dingus that affixes the trailer to the back of your motorcar. It is the coupling, and there are as many ideas about what it should be, and how it should work, as there are about how to be happy though married. There are short hitches and long hitches, cushioned hitches, and hitches with a universal joint. There are straight bar hitches and triangle hitches, and beak hitches and just plain bad-tempered, improvident, inefficient, malicious hitches, and we drew one of the latter.

Kelland's style was hyperbolic satire of the Mark Twain school: a blend of slapsticky humor and painful truth that can be immensely readable, immensely funny, to almost everyone but its victim. "How's Your Hitch?" infuriated the entire trailer industry; it erased the memory of every protrailer article the *Post* had ever run. For twenty years after-wards, industry members continued to blame Clarence Buddington Kelland and the *Post* for having nipped the 1930s trailer boom in the bud.

In truth, Kelland did little more than articulate the dark side of the trailer picture, the unromantic side that the mass of journalists had long ignored, and were only just beginning—in their reactionary, sour-grapes stage—to touch upon. Good parks *were* scarce in 1937, many trailers *were* under-engineered, and hitches (as well as heating stoves and brakes and taillights and roof ventilators and a hundred other things Kelland never mentions) *were* crude and sometimes trouble-some. For trailer builders and trailer users and trailer landlords as well, this was a pioneering period, and the day to day reality of any pioneer-ing period is always a far cry from the idyllic dreams that energize it.

In some respects, then, the satire in "How's Your Hitch?" was timely. It was about time that the journalists' myth of a carefree, tax-free, rent-free life on wheels was punctured. The sun, after all, doesn't shine perpetually on anyone, and there ain't, as people were fond of saying in those days, no free lunch. Certainly it was time to deflate the trailer industry's myth of an absolutely limitless future, of a shower of riches falling forever out of a hazy sky full of movie stars and industrialists and retired doctors and such.

But the deflation of these myths was at best peripheral to the in-dustry's crisis. There were far more tangible reasons, in late 1937, for the bursting of the trailer bubble. Out in the real world—the world of economics that surrounded and supported the trailer manufacturers' dream—another recession was beginning. All winter and spring, the auto industry had been plagued with a series of sit-down strikes by the newly formed United Auto Workers. And in the thirties, when the auto industry coughed, the rest of the country was sure to come down with the sniffles. Toward the end of summer, car dealers, many of whom were trailer dealers as well, began running out of inventory, confidence, and, finally, cashflow. All the indexes began to slide, and Americans who owned belts began once again to tighten them. The nation's econ-omy, after its long, slow climb back up from the depths of 1932, had started another helpless, heartbreaking spiral down into the abyss. Not surprisingly, it took the little trailer industry with it.

Even so, the trailermen might have kept their footing, might have hung on through this newest storm—it lasted some eighteen months— if only their market had been just half as strong as it appeared to be. But it wasn't. Although no one could see it at the time, the house trailer

"No one article could kill an industry."
—Jack Kneass, former editor of *Trail-R-News*

market, thanks to seven hundred or more active manufacturers, was beginning to saturate.

By the fall of 1937, not every American had a trailer who really wanted one, and not every trailer owner was wholly satisfied with his present coach. But the prospective customers now were fewer, and far more dollar conscious, than they had been since the boom began back in '35. No one could see it at the time, but 1937, disappointing though it was, would be the industry's biggest sales year until the coming of the war, when the house trailer would suddenly be needed more than wanted, and by a whole new class of trailerite, the wartimers, young and pragmatic and upwardly mobile, and pretty much immune to the old pioneer disease of trailer fever.

10 Masonite Mansions, Homasote Homes

Trailers, like jeeps, are an answer to a war demand, and don't pretend to be ideal.

Business Week,
July 1, 1943

I've got a dream house I'll build there someday,
With picket fence and ramblin' rose.

—popular song

In April of 1938, *Harper's Monthly* published a three-page essay on the trailer movement entitled "Epitaph for the Trailer Dream." It was one of those lofty and intellectual overviews—exactly the sort of detached, logical, dispassionate prose you expect from a highbrow magazine. But just beneath the article's unrippled surface flowed a strong undercurrent of sadness and disillusionment, a barely-concealed sense of loss. However casually you might skim through the piece, you couldn't help feeling that the writer was dealing with matters very near to his own heart.

The author was Philip H. Smith, one of a handful of journalists who had followed the house trailer's social progress ever since it emerged from the woods in 1935. Without ever owning a trailer himself, Smith had written enthusiastically about trailers for a number of magazines. The lovely and wickedly misleading phrase "go anywhere, stop anywhere, escape taxes and rent" was his, from a 1936 article in *Automotive Industries*. This sort of romantic posey might have endeared him to the trailer manufacturers, might even have caused one of them to snap him up for their sales and publicity department, except that Smith's ro-

"Perhaps you have been on a long motor trip and at the weariest part of the journey you've happened upon that billboard which says: 'If you lived here you'd be home now.' That is, perhaps, what gave rise to the trailer."
—Philip H. Smith, in *SAE Transactions*, February 1937

manticism was too often tempered with clear-headed, objective phrases like "the future of the trailer, of course, lies in its possibilities as a home"—phrases that made most of the manufacturers uncomfortable in those prewar years. But one thing was clear: Smith was bewitched by these little houses on wheels. He was, if not a trailerite, at least a fellow traveler, a man with more than a touch of trailer fever.

And now, in *Harper's*, he was writing the trailer's epitaph, and a small part of him seemed to be dying with it. But of course it wasn't the trailer itself that Smith was laying to rest, as he well knew. It was the trailer dream—the dream of freedom, of escape, of that more carefree and less mundane life that the rolling home had seemed at first to offer—the dream of a hillbilly heaven out there somewhere at the ragged edge of suburban America, E. B. White's "Garden of Eden on wheels." Smith seems personally let down by the trailer's failure to live up to the ballyhoo—some of which was his own—that had surrounded its birth.

"Take from no man his dream."
—*I Ching,* the Chinese Book of Changes

> "Think of it," Smith says in the "Epitaph," "by combining the housing characteristics of the snail with the speed of the antelope we were to lower the cost of living, acquire a boom business, take up the slack in employment, and solve the age-old problem of housing! We, the people, hoped for all that."

By 1938 it had become obvious to trailer watchers like Smith that mobile living was not destined to be the ultimate solution to America's problems, economic or otherwise. Just as obviously, half of America was never to live on wheels, as Roger Babson had so confidently predicted back in '35—or at least not the half that Philip Smith belonged to. Retirees and pensioners and teachers on sabbatical, people looking for work, artisans and craftsmen and salesmen whose skills were in high demand, seasonal laborers such as carnival workers and fruit pickers and harvesting crews, people with no children in school, people with itchy feet, people without strong ties to church and state, to social clubs and extended families—the more daring of these might escape into the gypsy life of trailerdom, might disappear forever into the inviting shade of the parks. But Smith, like most Americans, was not one of these, and he had finally come to admit it—in print, with a barely-concealed sigh. "Epitaph" was his last piece of trailer journalism.

Smith's sense of disillusionment with the trailer dream was shared by a great many people during 1937 and 1938. On editorial pages all across America, bitter antitrailer diatribes had begun to replace the paeans of praise. The trailer changed, almost overnight, from an excitingly portentous gadget to a nuisance, then a menace to health, and finally a threat to home and family, as whole legions of desk-bound dreamers and Underwood utopians recovered from their early, childlike infatuation with the trailer, and turned energetically to angry rejection and sour grapes. The trailer movement, like a new religion, moved forward in a storm of controversy. It polarized everyone's thinking: you were either for trailers, or else you were against them. Few people, at the time, seemed able to view the phenomenon dispassionately.

The intensity of the public backlash against trailering suggests something of the depth of America's need, in mid-Depression, for a new grail, a new public dream. When the trailer movement first came to national attention, in 1935, the country was still adrift, still reeling from the shock of the boom-and-bust twenties. Like the automobile of the teens, trailers seemed to promise both riches and escape. But unlike the automobile, the trailer couldn't deliver—not, at least, to any appreciable percentage of the populace. By 1937 it had been around long enough (not merely in the media, but in vacant lots and neighbors' yards and makeshift camps that reminded at least one writer of "the places where elephants go to die") so that only Hollywood—and the half-million or so victims of trailer fever—could seriously imagine that life in these little boxes might really be heaven on wheels.

The widespread sense of paradise lost, of having been tantalized by an impossible dream, helped to fuel the legal backlash against trailering that began about this time. For two years, from the spring of 1937 to the summer of 1939, a veritable cloudburst of laws rained down on the trailerites' heads. Cities that didn't ban them completely relegated trailer parks to their ugliest and noisiest industrial zones—jammed them down, typically, between a crowded expressway and a thriving railroad line. Others passed their scram laws designed to discourage long-term trailer living, while still others attempted blatant overtaxation

"An engineer said he did not believe that the [trailer] campers would be bothered by the screeching of whistles or the rumbling of trains over the New York Central tracks that bound the east side of the camp."
—*The New York Times*, September 3, 1937

of the little vehicles, a movement that culminated in San Diego's short-lived "dime-a-day" trailer tax of 1942. All of these laws, punitive and discriminatory though they obviously were, required lengthy court battles to overturn.

Much of this harassment the trailerites themselves could escape by taking to their wheels—by moving, as suggested earlier, just outside corporate jurisdiction. But these were dark days for the manufacturers, whose already shaky business was threatened by every new law, every piece of negative publicity. Between the fall of 1937 and the spring of 1940, hundreds of smaller companies folded, while many of the bigger manufacturers merged and diversified and sold off assets in frantic attempts to stay in business.

Covered Wagon, the industry's flagship for eight years, found itself in the spring of 1938 with chassis and running gear pouring in the front door at the rate of one hundred units a day, while its sales slipped to five or ten units a day. Barely twelve months after its first stock issue, Covered Wagon went into bankruptcy and reorganization. Though Sherman continued to produce trailers right up until the war, even introducing, in early '39, a conventionally streamlined Residential Model, Covered Wagon never really recovered from the disastrous fall of 1937. Its smaller and more flexible competitors, those who were lucky enough to survive the recession, split Sherman's market share half a dozen ways and never gave much of it back. By late 1938, the trailer business seemed to have collapsed back into the little side street garages and furniture shops from which it had sprung.

Early in 1940, however, the wheel of fortune turned once more, and the few remaining manufacturers found themselves once again in a growth industry. For Europe had plunged itself into another war, just as it had in 1914, and America had again vowed, in the words of George Washington, to "steer clear of foreign entanglements," just as it had in 1914. But America wasn't averse to turning a profit on these foreign entanglements—it had done well in the first great war—and so its defense industries began gearing up to supply England and her allies with matériel, while its government began gearing up to lend them the dollars to buy with. And a second trailer boom got quietly under way.

Not that England and her allies needed American house trailers to fight Hitler's war. But American defense workers—and America's growing ranks of military personnel—desperately needed places to live during what was quickly labeled, on this side of the Atlantic, "the emergency."

Emergency housing. Temporary housing. Almost anyone could accept trailer life under those terms. You didn't have to be a real trailerite, didn't have to have the least symptom of trailer fever, to appreciate having a plywood roof over your head during "the emergency," especially if you happened to be hundreds of miles from home and family, making good money at some place like the giant new powder plant down on the Ohio River near Charlestown, Indiana, where, in the fall of 1940, eleven hundred men were sleeping in their automobiles because there wasn't so much as a leaky toolshed within sixty miles that wasn't already caulked and whitewashed and rented out.

For the surviving trailer builders, "the emergency" did more than balance their checkbooks. It also had the effect of clearing the air—and the manufacturers' consciences. At last they could drop the silly pretense that their vehicles were mostly vacation toys for the wealthy. At last they could openly acknowledge that almost all of the industry's design efforts since 1935 had been to create, not camping trailers, not vehicles for recreation, but more livable miniature homes. At last they could admit that their little coaches were getting longer and heavier and more awkward every year because, in the largely blue-collar housing market they were serving, livability took precedence over roadability. (For a true camping trailer, such as the all-aluminum Bowlus Road Chief or its sleek imitator, the Airstream Clipper, this formula was quite obviously reversed.) At last they could hold their heads up in society: their products, their house trailers, were not merely rolling slums for the unshaven masses. Now they were desperately needed defense housing for "the emergency."

And at last the truth became apparent: during the prewar decade, no one in America had been more snobbish, more prejudiced against the pioneer trailerite than the trailer manufacturers themselves—especially the manufacturers in the land yacht class, like Fleetwheels-Coates president Charles F. de Ganahl, whose wife confided to *Trailer*

"But for the most part the trailer has proved a useful and reasonably comfortable solution [to the problem] of living quarters for the nomadic worker in the present emergency."
—*The New York Times*, June 29, 1941

Topics, after a cross-country trip in 1937, that "trailerites are a much better class of people than I was led to expect by our Florida observations."

The long, heavy, overpriced trailer that de Ganahl produced was a true snob mobile, an imitation Curtiss Aerocar—ten thousand dollars worth of leather-lined luxury, built expressly for shuttling the wealthy back and forth to Florida; and so the good lady might be forgiven her exaggerated sense of self. But her arrogance was shared, though seldom expressed so baldly, by most of the mass-market builders, as well. The major manufacturers had all tried at one time or another to distance themselves from the real trailerites, the full-timers, with their shirt-sleeve society, their flapping laundry, and their constant problems with city ordinances. And this despite the fact that, as Jim Brown loved to point out, these folk—these cranky and independent full-timers—formed the bulk of the house trailer market, and always had.

But now it was 1940, and "the emergency" was in full swing. America's trailermen were ready to put all that snobbery, all that hopeful pretense, behind them. They were ready, at last, to come to terms with the most fundamental, and embarrassing, fact of their existence, a fact they had tried to hide ever since the industry came of age: for every William Vanderbilt who owned a trailer, there were a thousand—maybe ten thousand—Hildred Gumarsols.

The Vanderbilts made news; the Gumarsols, except in rare cases like the Orchard Lake lawsuit, did not. The Vanderbilts were rich and elegant; the Gumarsols were neither. The Vanderbilts were articulate: Cornelius, Jr., a veteran trailer tripper since childhood, was a frequent contributor of articles to the trailering magazines, and even chaired, during 1938, a short-lived national owners' organization. The Gumarsols of the trailer movement, by contrast, tended to be inarticulate, hard to organize, hard even to reach: a typical amorphous American consumer group, scattered thinly across the hinterlands.

As early as 1937, two years into the trailer boom, there were three national trailering magazines, and of course they all claimed to reach, through their numerous reader surveys, every category of trailer user. For the most part, they did not. For the most part, they reached only the Vanderbilts—the trailer enthusiasts, the part-timers, the weekenders, the sort of sport trailerites who form the bulk of the recreational

"During the past three or four years approximately 75% of the trailer coaches manufactured have been sold for semi-permanent homes."
—TCMA president James L. Brown, *Trailer Topics,* December 1940

vehicle market today. The great mass of full-timers, scattered across America in back yards and vacant lots and working-class courts, the trailer magazines seldom touched.

My parents were probably a bit more literate than the average full-time trailerite of the thirties and forties. Both of them read voraciously, and a constant stream of books and magazines and newspapers flowed through our household as I was growing up. Yet I never saw a trailering magazine, wasn't even aware of their existence, until long after I was grown, long after I'd ceased to live on wheels. And I suspect that my experience was typical. The people who made their homes in trailers didn't need to read about trailering any more than a fish needs to read about water. Trailer magazines were for dreamers and dilettantes, for weekenders.

When the new models came out in the late fall, my father would get the word through the park grapevine, or see the newspaper ads. The next Saturday we'd pile into our car and go tire kicking—drive in to Houston, Denver, Fort Wayne or Dayton or Tuscaloosa, depending on where we were living at the time, for the big dealers were always in the cities, the parks always in the suburbs and small towns and bedroom communities nearby. Most of America's trailerites were either retirees or, like my family, a part of that great Hildred Gumarsol blue-collar working-class—the people that the manufacturers had been pretending didn't exist.

"Most cities prefer that you remain on the outskirts. This pleases the trailer owner; you don't have to tell him to avoid the city; it's the very thing he's trying to get away from."
—*Trailer Topics,*
June 1939

But now, thanks to "the emergency," the working class was suddenly coming up in the world, suddenly worthy of acknowledgment. As the defense plants began to whirr, all these blue-collar people became, almost overnight, national assets, and the trailer builders didn't have to be ashamed of them any more. "Are these good folk needing a place to live? Why, tell 'em to step right this way—I do believe we got exactly what they're looking for."

A few of the trailermen enjoyed a quiet chuckle from this sudden industry about-face. One was Wilbur Schult, the Indiana haberdasher-turned-trailermaker who had once had the bad taste to admit to a journalist that he got his start in trailer building, in 1934, by selling to "circus people and other itinerant workers" who saw the big Schult billboards around Elkhart and came in for a free factory tour. Jim Brown, of course, was another. A tireless fighter for trailerite rights,

Brown had, by 1940, risen to the presidency of the Trailer Coach Manufacturers Association, the first nonmanufacturer to head the group. Brown had seen through the vacation trailer sham right from the start and was pleased that it was over; now the industry could get on with its true calling, which was the designing and building of portable housing.

Not everyone thought the new honesty was a blessing, though. Out in Los Angeles, Airstream founder Wally Byam was enraged. For years he had maintained, at the top of his voice, that his Airstreams were campers, not homes, and he didn't approve of them being used otherwise. When the emergency began, Byam stuck to his guns. He could have thrown in with the pack and started building what he loudly derided as "substandard housing on wheels." But he didn't. He closed the doors at Airstream, instead, and went to work for Lockheed Aircraft. Wally Byam, depending on whom you talk to, was either the most pigheaded man in the entire trailer business, or else the most principled.

"Transformation of the trailer from a roving householder's vehicle to a source of defense housing and military rolling stock has been sudden and unintentional with the industry."
—*Business Week,*
December 7, 1940

So the trailer industry, or what was left of it after the '37–'38 recession, was already backordered by the boom in private defense housing when, in late November of 1940, a brand-new customer came knocking on its door: the federal government. Uncle Sam needed 1,500 "living" trailers, pronto. No, wait, make that 6,500. When could he expect them?

The little industry was stunned. Sixty-five hundred trailers—almost six months worth of production, at the modest 1940 rate of twelve to fifteen thousand trailers a year. And this was over and above all those fresh dealer orders already hanging on the peg. The trailermen went into a huddle, began to take stock of themselves. Could they possibly organize to meet this challenge? Were they really an industry, or just a handful of jealous carpenters fighting over a small and extremely volatile market? True, they'd been able to pull together under the TCMA banner back in '36, and they'd battled a few unfair laws with fair success. But that was the good old days, when the industry was booming and the trailer market had seemed limitless. Then came the year of the locust, and it very nearly wiped the slate clean. The TCMA itself had only just survived. Even now, it spoke for no more than twenty of the largest eastern and midwestern manufacturers. What about all the little builders scattered around the country who didn't belong? Could they be trusted to help with this huge government order? Should they be asked? And, more specifically, what about all those trailer builders out in southern California?

Oh, that southern California! Do we have to talk about southern California?

Like the state of Texas, the bottom half of the Bear Flag State has never really belonged wholeheartedly to the one nation, indivisible. And America at large has always been of two minds about the place. Is it a dream come true, or simply a peculiarly American nightmare? Should we envy its balmy skies and orange groves, or laugh at its wild excesses? Is the vast and smog-washed Los Angeles basin really the land of tomorrow, or just America's permanent carnival midway, a kind of freak show without end? Sunny southern California! A world of freedom without bounds—or taste. Should we vote it out of the Union? Or sell the house this fall and move out there where the action is?

And southern Californians—those mystical millions who actually inhabit that artificial greenbelt between the Mojave and the Pacific— have traditionally responded to this massive ambivalence with an equally massive indifference. If everything east of the Sierras slid off into the Atlantic Ocean tonight, nobody in Greater Los Angeles would so much as notice. Not, at least, until the Colorado dried up and spoiled their weekend at Havasu.

This polarization of feeling isn't new. It was alive and well as far back as the turn of the century, when a group of southern California automobilists, feeling themselves isolated from the Chicago-based American Autombile Association, got together and formed their own little version of the Triple A. They called it the Automobile Club of Southern California, and it was not, repeat *not*, an AAA affiliate. One of the first things the AC of SC did was to totally eclipse the AAA— not to mention the entire U.S. government—by mapping and sign-posting a set of narrow, dusty wheel ruts that ran east out of Los Angeles all the way to the Atlantic Ocean. In doing so they created, single-handedly, the first clearly-marked, all-weather transcontinental motor route right to the door of their own home town, which, naturally, profited in no small measure from their efforts. Today, both town and auto club are still growing—and both are still pretty much indifferent to the "easterners" of the AAA.

Not surprisingly, a similar pattern of separate-but-equal developed in the trailer business. At about the time the Trailer Coach Manufacturers Association was forming in the Midwest, a handful of builders began meeting once a month for lunch at Clifton's Cafeteria in downtown Los Angeles, right under a sign on the wall saying that if you didn't have any money, you didn't have to pay—a small reminder that even in the land of milk and honey the Depression was far from over in 1936. This little group of western trailermen called themselves the Trailer Coach Manufacturers Association of California (a name they soon shortened to the Trailer Coach Association—TCA—in order to include distributors, dealers, and park owners and, no doubt, to distinguish themselves from the other TCMA.) Right from the start, the TCA and the TCMA began talking about getting together, about forming one strong, unified, national organization. And they did, too—thirty-nine years later, in 1975. Which all goes to show that it's a long way from Chicago to Los Angeles, and it always has been.

But eastern and western trailermen of the 1930s were divided by more than mere geography and regional chauvinism. They had basic philosophical differences, as well. Out in sunny California, before World War II, the automobile trailer actually was the play vehicle that the builders in the East claimed it to be. Out in sunny California, strangely enough, a lot of people took their cue from the movie stars and bought trailers just for a lark. Oh, a few thousand Californians moved into them permanently—why not, in such a mild climate?—but until around 1940, until "the emergency" was well under way, the percentage of full-timers on the West Coast was far lower than elsewhere in the country. Why? Had Californians already escaped, so that they had no need for this alternative way of living? Did California's huge influx of dust-bowl immigrants during the middle thirties—the "Okies" with their sad little homemade shack trailers—tarnish the image of life on wheels for the whole West Coast? Or did the inexpensive "California bungalow" simply compete too successfully with the house trailer in price?

For whatever the reason, California trailer builders faced a very dif-

"Few will deny, we think, that housing standards are consistently higher in Southern California than in most Eastern and Midwestern sectors. It simply costs less to build a liveable house here—much less."
—*Westways*, January 1938

ferent market from the one back East. Theirs was largely a sport market, a market composed of hunters and fishermen and vacationers and weekend woodsmen. And so, right from the start, California-built trailers tended to be smaller and lighter, more nimble and less sophisticated, than "eastern" coaches—much closer in philosophy to the sprightly little English caravan than to the bulky house trailers of the Chicago-based TCMA. And because they were chiefly playthings, built for occasional use in a perennially mild climate, most of the prewar California trailers were, to put it kindly, underinsulated.

But these little underinsulated marvels had perfectly good wheels beneath them, and so they didn't always stay in California. Some of them wandered east and north, into climates where palm trees fear to tread, climates they were never intended to handle. And people in these climates bought them, and moved into them, and tried to stay warm inside them—tried, and invariably failed. With two-inch-thick walls full of nothing but dead air, these California-built trailers tended to sweat inside during cold weather—sweat, and then, late at night after the stove went out, freeze. It was not unusual, in one of these early TCA rigs, for a woman to wake up before sunrise with her hair frozen to the plywood wall next to the bed. This was not heaven on wheels.

> "Of course, those of us on the West Coast didn't have to build against blizzards and sub-zero weather."
> —Omar Suttles, Airfloat founder

As a consequence, the Los Angeles trailermen got an undeserved reputation in the rest of the country for jerry building—a reputation that clung to them throughout the entire trailerite era. There were some excellent house trailers built in California before the war, all-weather coaches like the Roadhome Pullman and the larger Masterbilt models, trailers that were designed specifically for long-term living. But the thousands of lightweight camping rigs that were the TCA's bread and butter were what easterners like my father tended to think of as "California trailers." My dad would get just close enough to a new coach to read the TCA on the label, then throw up his nose like a goat. "California-built!" he'd snort, and turn away without a second look. He would do this even when we were living and shopping in Los Angeles.

By the late forties this prejudice was outdated, for the war had drawn a sharp line between the travel trailer and the house trailer; by 1943 no manufacturer, and few buyers, would ever confuse the two again. But my father cherished his TCA/TCMA distinction—perhaps as a form

Prewar California trailers were mostly lightweight camping rigs. Only a few, like this distinctive caravan-style Masterbilt, were fully insulated and equipped for long-term living.

of loyalty to the Midwest of his childhood—and carried it with him to his grave. Certainly it saved the family a lot of tire kicking each time the new models came out.

"The emergency" that began with Hitler's invasion of Poland in '39 dragged on for over two years. Then, in December of '41, Tojo's warplanes screamed out of the sky over Pearl Harbor and put an end to American euphemism: the country was officially at war. And suddenly plywood, canvas, glass, copper, steel, rubber—all the materials of trailer building—were needed for ships and planes and tanks. Priority lists began to appear in the newspapers, and house trailers were not on them; house trailers were not considered war matériel.

Trailermen instantly saw the flaw in this thinking. Housing shortages, for both military and civilian personnel, could only worsen. It took about a thousand man-hours to build a conventional house, and only 112 man-hours to build a house trailer. Because trailers were assembled indoors, older and less physically fit workers could do the job. And most importantly, trailer housing wasn't permanent and wouldn't create ghost towns like the ones that plagued manufacturing centers after World War I. When the war was over and the trailerite work force left town, they could take their houses with them.

These arguments made sense, and the government ultimately listened. Through the National Housing Agency it began to order trailers by the thousand, but with this stipulation: they had to be designed around a maximum of 275 pounds of steel and three pounds of cop-

An artist's rendition of an actual trailer park shows the resemblance to the Levittowns and other developments which sprouted up across America following World War II. But not even commercial artists could bring themselves to look at mobile homes: some of these caricatures sit backwards in their spaces; some have barn doors; others have no doors at all. Chef Menteur indeed! (Photo courtesy Curt Teich Postcard Archives.)

BEACON TRAILER PARK

4440 CHEF MENTEUR HY. ON U. S. 90   NEW ORLEANS. LA.

per—less than a quarter of the metal normally needed. What about plywood? What about masonite? the builders asked. Good luck, they were told.

The unfortunate result was the "war" or "government" trailer—the cardboard trailer of 1942–43. Framed in cheap pine, covered on the outside with a soft insulation board called "homasote" (a mixture of wood pulp and ground newsprint), covered on the inside with upson board, a kind of pale and water-soluable homasote, these war trailers— over 38,000 of them—were delivered to sites on wheels and axles borrowed from a government pool, slipped onto temporary founda- tions, and rented, for a dollar a day, to anyone who could prove their presence was needed to help defeat Hitler and Tojo.

Off-base military families swarmed into these little paper boxes by the score. Defense plant workers shared them, husbands and wives packing lunches simultaneously in the narrow kitchen and then car pooling away together, often as not, to work the same shift. It has been estimated that the government trailer alone exposed more than a hundred thousand American families to trailer life.

Unfortunately, the experience was too often a bleak one. The parks set up for these cardboard wonders were almost uniformly grim: a few muddy, regimented acres just outside some industrial plant gate, with- out a tree, without a blade of grass, without a single redeeming feature except a gas-saving proximity to the workplace. Row upon row of identical army brown trailers, looking like burnt cookies on a baking sheet. No patios. No awnings. Shared washrooms and laundry rooms, sometimes conventionally-built structures, sometimes nothing more than cardboard trailers themselves. World War II in the defense parks meant mud in the winter, dust in the summer, gasoline rationing, meat rationing, coffee rationing, and long lines at the toilets. What a life.

Not everyone saw it this way. Californian Edythe Bordwell has noth- ing but good memories of her two years on the largest trailer park, government or private, in history. This monster park was located, not in southern Florida—no such luck—but out on the windy, sun-baked, snow-blown flats of eastern Washington, just up the Columbia River from Richland, at the top-secret Hanford Reactor Site. Bordwell and her husband bought a trailer, a small, homemade job, and moved there in early 1944, trading up to a larger model but staying put until "the

spring after Hiroshima." The friendliness and cleanliness of the place
still remains in her memory.

The Hanford park was unbelievably large. When the tin can tourists
would pour into Tampa or Bradenton or Sarasota for winter convention
during the late thirties, over a thousand car and trailer rigs might
bivouac in a single park. But at Hanford, in 1944–45, more than four
thousand trailers occupied a single site: a wheeled city of some twelve
thousand souls, right out beside the reactor buildings on a treeless
plain of tumbleweed and sagebrush. Managed by Dupont Chemical,
the prime contractor at Hanford, the park had steam-heated bathhouses
("Immaculate," Bordwell recalls), a movie theater, and its own newspaper, the *Sage Sentinel,* full of sage admonitions about not mailing any
copies out of the park. For the Hanford trailer city, like the rest of the
atomic facility, simply did not exist, officially. Not until the war was
over and the four thousand rigs were scattered to the winds did word
of the world's largest, and bleakest, trailer park leak out.

But hardship, even more than other shared experiences, breaks
down the walls that separate us, and thousands of friendships bloomed
and faded in these government camps. Baptists from Waycross, Georgia
talked for the first time to Mormons from Provo, and found each other
much alike. Neighbors traded ration stamps and rides to the grocery
store, babysat each other's children, brought food to the sick and gifts
to the newborn, rallied around one another to share the happiness of
good news and support the grief of bad. Families moved in and out
much as they had on peacetime parks, though the cardboard trailers
themselves tended to stay put until the war was over due to a shortage
of wheels and axles. Perched on sawhorses or simple block foundations,
these war trailers were really not trailers at all, in any true sense.
Stripped of their wheels, they were reduced to mere apartments, and
crude ones at that, little better than shacks, with none of the mobility
or promise of freedom of a conventional house trailer.

Almost every defense park would contain, in addition to the rentals,
a scattering of privately-owned trailers—trailers built and bought before the war, "real" trailers, with running gear intact. Oddly cheerful
creatures, these private models, with their two-tone leatherette or masonite hulls, their immense sixteen-by-thirty-two-inch windows (the
government models, due to glass shortages, had little pinchy ones) and

Douglas Dam, Tennessee, June 1942. The bleakness of wartime parks drew people together, often into lifelong friendships.

their rich, wood-grained interiors. What a delight to step into one of these private rigs after living for months in a government coach! Once you got over the shock of all that golden wood veneer, the first thing you noticed were the electrical outlets: plugs for irons, plugs for toasters, plugs for lamps, plugs everywhere! (Government trailers had only one outlet: three pounds of copper, remember.) And lights! Wall lamps and dome lights and a light over the sink and yet another one over the stove—more lights than Broadway! And just look at the size of that sink, won't you, and cupboards enough for two weeks' groceries!

Mobile home historians like to say that people's experience in the government trailers during the war helped fuel the postwar trailer boom. It seems just as likely that it fueled the new-housing boom, instead. It's hard to conceive of anything that might make a person crave high, wasteful ceilings and huge picture windows and central heating and hardwood floors quite as much as being cooped up for the duration in a rented upson-board cubicle, seven by eighteen feet inside, with no bathroom—no running water at all, often as not—with the same linoleum on the countertops as on the floors, with almost no windows, and only a single electrical outlet.

The trailer pioneers, the people like my parents who owned rigs before Pearl Harbor, were better prepared for the war than most other Americans. Already accustomed to following the labor market—jobs and rumors of jobs—wherever it might lead, the terrible dislocations of wartime seemed perfectly normal to them. Among them were a high proportion of skilled and semiskilled craftsmen, people who virtually had their pick of jobs during the first year or so of the war. Then new construction slowed, the economy settled into its war production phase, and many, like my father, had to learn new skills: the feisty little Ohio bricklayer became a supply man at an army aviation depot, with a head full of part numbers for the B–25 bomber.

An immediate result of the war was that the number of parks around defense and military centers doubled and tripled, while those in "non-defense areas," meaning 90 percent of the country, lost their trade and went into steep decline. The government run parks kept their rents down, but it was a seller's market, and private parks tended to charge what the traffic would bear.

And, predictably, the quality of park life fell off. With facilities habitually overcrowded, and so little lumber, glass, concrete and even paint available for expansion or repair, wash houses and restrooms grew shabby and neglected, potholes nibbled at the park drives, fences sagged, and landscaping withered and died. City ordinances that limited a trailer's length of stay—the so-called scram laws—were almost universally suspended during the war and seldom reinstated afterwards, and this was a quiet victory for the trailerites. But along with such ordinances, many of the strict sanitation rules that had been passed to govern the camps in the late thirties went unenforced as well, and a lot of landlords took advantage of this laxity. Sewers backed up, garbage areas overflowed, rainwater collected in puddles. Even the best parks went downhill during the war.

Far too many trailerites were willing to accept crude and unsanitary living conditions as necessary for the war effort. A large percentage of

"When the war broke out they was calling for welders down in San Diego and up in Bremerton, both. My wife said we'd already lived in San Diego, and she wanted to see Puget Sound. It didn't make me any difference, so we went to Bremerton and stayed there two years."
—pioneer trailerite E. L. Shannon, 78, in conversation, Chico, California, 1988

them were merely wartimers, trailer dwellers with no real investment in the culture, people who were only in the parks because they could find no other housing, who were just camping out for the duration, making good money and squirreling it away to buy a "real" home as soon as peace broke out. This wartime complacency—on the part of the full-timers as well as wartimers—established precedents for the slum parks of the postwar era, the era of high-class parks and low-class parks, and not much in between.

In this respect the war was a setback to the serious, long-term trailerite, for afterwards the full-timers had to start all over in the long, slow game of pressuring landlords to upgrade their facilities. And at first it was a losing battle, for a third trailer boom, beginning in 1946, poured a new generation of coaches into the already overcrowded parks, keeping space rental at a premium, just as it had been during the war. But how long would this new boom last? Could park developers trust so fickle and unstable a population, a people given to moving at the drop of a hat? Could they count on the trailerite to support new and expensive facilities? A few took the gamble, but the vast majority simply held onto their old, run-down, prewar parks, waiting to see what tomorrow might bring. Perhaps they were smart, as it turned out, for what tomorrow brought was the end of an era.

11 The Last House Trailer

And we'll all pass the bottle when the good fight's won.
—*popular song, 1862*

The sixth largest city in the United States is on wheels.
—*Newsweek, August 25, 1952*

With the return of peace in 1945, Americans began to cast about for the lost fragments of their lives. Where were we when the world fell apart four years ago? Who were we then? Who are we now?

For my parents, full-time trailerites since 1940, the release from war work and wartime park life—bleak and pinched and squalid—meant the chance to be free gypsies once more, to slip out from under the northern pall and live in sunshine all year round. Not long after V-J Day they hitched up, shook all the neighbors' hands, and rolled out exuberantly, bound once more for the Gulf Coast. On the way through Dallas, a sailor with a roll of hundred-dollar bills made a pass at their little Schult, and, impulsively, they sold it to him on the spot. They went on to Galveston in the LaSalle and spent the winter as renters, then returned to Ohio in early spring and bought a fifty-two-acre farm just outside of Cincinnati. Selling their trailer, buying a farm: these were acts of armistice madness, pure and simple. Did they really think they were settling down?

Both of them worked all summer renovating the old farmhouse, and in late fall, when the oaks and maples were at their most colorful, they resold the property at a good profit and invested their riches in a brand-new car and trailer. Sanity had returned. By the time the snow began to fall in the Ohio Valley that year, our little family was riding at anchor down in warm, sunny Tuscaloosa, listening, through the new rig's open

155

windows, to teenagers playing "I Wanna Go Back to Kokomo, Indiana" on the park jukebox. None of the three of us wanted anything of the kind.

The whole country had this same air of open-ended craziness right after the war. Everyone seemed to be rushing about trying to remember exactly where home was, and whether Thomas Wolfe had been right in saying that you can't go there again. The trailerites, those million-plus Americans with wheels under their kitchens, had a decided edge in this nationwide game of musical chairs. All across the country, trailer parks filled and emptied overnight: "Arthur says it's too hot here— we're gonna try Maine." America had shrunk during the war. A thousand miles was no longer a serious move—suddenly it was just an easy two-day pull, with a stop overnight beside some friendly gas station.

Long before the last troopship came home, the play parks of the Deep South—those surf-side parks destined to become the retirement complexes of the sixties and seventies and eighties—found themselves once again swamped with young families, as they had been before the war. And in all the parks, north, south, east, and west, the mild abrasions between the generations began all over again: the people without children asking to be separated from people with, the people who came to life, vampirelike, at 10:00 P.M. getting on the nerves of the folk who were winding their bedside clocks about then.

The great virtue of trailering, of course, was its mobility: no matter how eccentric a family's habits, there was bound to be a park further down the road that would accept them, a group of kindred spirits somewhere with an empty space in their midst. They had only to hitch up and roll out and keep looking till they found it.

This was the era of my childhood on the parks, and it was not a lonely childhood. An acute postwar housing shortage, coupled with the baby boom, filled the country's twenty thousand trailer encampments to overflowing with kids. It was an era of rising affluence, when the coaches themselves seemed to grow, like corn, in the night, partly because the families within them were growing so fast, and partly because, well, just because the neighbors were buying a bigger rig, and so why shouldn't we? The money, or at least the credit, was there, and a bigger trailer meant each family member could have a bit more of the one thing trailer life had never yet offered in any real abundance: personal privacy.

It was an accepted fact of trailering that personal space was at a premium. In bad weather especially, everyone would be driven inside. In bad weather, there was no running off to the beach to fish, to the laundry room or the corner grocery or the playground. Even the patio, under its striped awning, offered little protection against a sharp north wind, a driving rain. At such times only the trailer's living room, seven-and-a-half by ten, was warm and dry and inviting, and it was here that everyone retreated—to sew, to read, to mend fishing tackle, to play games, to laugh and tease and question and share. In inclement weather, living in a house trailer, you could not escape being a family.

If park life tested the trailerite's capacity for communal living, the trailer itself tested his need for solitude and withdrawal. Personal privacy had to be found outside the home—in work, in libraries, in nature, in hobbies and pastimes. If you grew tired of being with other people, grew tired of smiling and nodding sociably, grew tired of half-listening to their conversations, of hearing them click their teeth or chew their gum, if you simply wanted some time alone, you couldn't go to your room and close the door, for in the early trailers there was no room and no door.

Along in the late forties, as the trailers began to lengthen, back bedrooms became more common, master bedrooms that were cut off from the kitchen/living room space by closets and a bathroom and a narrow hallway with a sliding door. Back bedrooms were where you escaped to read when the front room was too full of life. Back bedrooms were where the kids were sent to play when families came visiting on rainy days. Two separate and reasonably noisy worlds could coexist under the same narrow roof, thanks to that long hallway and its sliding door.

The prewar trailers, the pioneer rigs, were really too short for this division into separate rooms, though they sometimes had curtains provided for that purpose. There was barely enough room in a prewar model for harmony, almost never enough for anger. Fortunately, most of the trailer pioneers, like my parents, were of stoic northern European stock, people who had made the transition from house to trailer with

"People'd say, 'Doncha get clausterphoby living in that thing?' Now, how can you get clausterphoby when you're never more'n three feet from a window?"
—former trailerite John Fee, 74, in conversation, 1988

"More than two in a trailer does not make for comfortable living."
—*Trailer Topics,* January 1938

Trailer living rooms, seldom larger than seven by ten feet, were the center of family life—especially in bad weather. Couches usually sat across the front of the room, but this family has moved theirs to the side.

most of their inhibitions intact. Screaming matches in the early parks were, by all accounts, rare.

Once, before I was born, my parents got into an argument over one of those half-million things that two stubborn, middle-aged newlyweds might disagree upon, and my father stomped out of their little Schult in anger. My mother fumed about inside for awhile, and then decided to take the bus downtown to go shopping for the afternoon. As she was changing into her town dress she suddenly heard my father's footsteps on the patio. There she stood, in her slip, still seething, and she knew one thing for certain: dressed or undressed, she did not want to deal with that man. So she stepped quickly into the clothes closet—the bathroom was too far away to reach—and pulled the door to.

My father came in, glanced about, and, not seeing her, decided she must have gone out. So he sat down at the table, pulled out a deck of cards, and played a slow hand of solitaire. And then another. Less than six feet away, my mother huddled silently in the tiny closet, gritting her teeth. My dad lit his pipe, relaxed, dealt another hand—the day was young. My mother shut her eyes and clenched her fists, standing like a warm poker in the darkness, hardly daring to breathe. Slap. Slap. Slap. She heard each card hit the table slowly, deliberately, thoughtfully.

Books have been written about the game of solitaire. There are more variations of this single game than there are all other card games combined, and so, not surprisingly, it is the most widely played card game in the world. The British, who were playing a similar game over two centuries ago with little cards less than two inches on a side, have another name for it. They call it "patience."

Slap. Slap. Slap.

After perhaps an hour, perhaps closer to two, my father got slowly to his feet, put the deck back in its box and put the box away—everything in its place—and then moved past the closet and into the kitchen to fix himself a sandwich. His left elbow, as he worked at the sink counter, more than once bumped the thin veneer wall behind which my mother stood. Probably he didn't notice that the closet door was ajar. If he had, he would almost certainly have reached over and shut it: everything in its place. The latch was a sturdy one, designed to keep the door from flying open in transit, and of course it was on the outside—you couldn't work it from within.

But he didn't notice the unlatched door, and so he didn't reach over and shut it. Instead, he lit the stove, reheated the breakfast coffee, poured himself a cup, and sat back down at the table with his sandwich to complete whatever meditation he had begun over the cards.

Like solitaire, eating takes little concentration; it's a time for staring into inner space, a time for burying the past and digging up the future. My mother, standing in the closet for well over two hours now, was beginning to run out of anger. Her legs and back ached. The coffee smelled wonderful. She bit her lip and swallowed her pride, and was just on the verge of pushing open the closet door when, abruptly, my father got up, rinsed his coffee cup in the sink, and went outside. He clumped noisily across the wooden patio, got into the La Salle, and drove off. At this point my mother stepped out of the closet, stretched herself back to full height, finished dressing, had a leisurely cup of coffee and took the bus downtown. This happened in 1941, and I first heard the story in the early fifties. I do not know when my father first heard it.

"Dirty dishes are ten times worse in a trailer than they are in a kitchen."
—*Trailer Topics*, May 1939

Donald Cowgill took many of the notes for his 1941 book, *Mobile Homes*, while he and his family were vacationing in their trailer. More than once in the book he bemoans the lack of privacy for writing and thinking and "taking stock of one's self."

"Some of us," Cowgill notes, "find it difficult to find time and the privacy for such occasions in the bustle of ordinary urban living. Much more difficult is it to maintain one's integrity in the close association of trailer life."

It's probably safe to say that trailerite men felt this lack of privacy, this lack of alone time, even more than women. Most women of the postwar era didn't work outside the home, so they had the trailer pretty much to themselves all day, while their husbands were at work and the children in school. Much as they might socialize over the washtubs, or over cards and coffee, there was still time in the average day for writing and thinking and taking stock of oneself.

But house trailers lacked both garage and basement, the two traditional male retreats. I recall men who carried fairly complete miniature tool shops right in the trunk of their car—tools for building bread boards and birdhouses and toys and cup racks and all those little projects from the back pages of *Popular Mechanics*. Sitting in a canvas lawn chair shaded by an open car trunk, or sometimes up on the patio beneath the awning, they would whittle and saw and sand and paint, making a mechanical goose that flapped its plywood wings in the breeze, making a wooden nameplate for a trailer window, making a varnished box shaped like a miniature outhouse to protect a barometer from the rain—only to give the finished object away to a neighbor down the row, someone they might never see again. Obviously pleased

with their handiwork, these patio craftsmen were not especially attached to the thing itself. They seemed happy just in the solitary creation of it.

There were men who read the newspaper in the washrooms, latching
the painted plywood door and tying up a toilet stall for an hour or
more on Saturday mornings. As a kid I used to think constipation must
be a real problem for adults, but now I understand: these men simply
needed some alone time. The washrooms, in the southern parks, at
least, were airy, whitewashed cubicles with high ceilings, scrubbed and
disinfected so often that the smell of PineSol still takes me back there;
not unpleasant places, on the whole, for reading the paper. Other men
would spend a long time in the shower stalls, singing or humming
quietly to themselves, wasting gallons and gallons of water in those
days before anyone outside of Death Valley thought it precious, letting
the roar of the shower head and the thin white linen curtain shut out
the world.

My father found his solace in fishing. Home from a long day's work
on some noisy and demanding construction job, he would sit patiently
through the family dinner, trading school news, park news, and job
news with wife and son. And then—not every evening, but just when
he needed it—he'd rig one of the deep-sea poles he kept, broken down,
in the trunk of the car, throw his hip waders over his shoulder, and
walk to the beach to fish alone in the Gulf. He always hunted with
friends, and later with his son, but he preferred to do his fishing alone.
Standing patiently, silently, waist-deep in the Gulf's gentle rollers
seemed to restore his soul, and he would return to the park after sunset
to distribute his catch and spend the rest of the evening reading, talking, joking, visiting with neighbors, playing cribbage or solitaire and
being his public self once again.

Some people, even as children, are more aware of their need for
privacy and personal space than others. One woman of my acquain-
tance, an instructor at the University of California at Berkeley, shared
a small trailer during the war years with three adults and two other
young children, a sister and a cousin. Although the trailer had a cabana
room attached, there was still too little privacy for a bookish ten-year-
old. "I used to go out and sit in the car just to be alone," she remembers.
"My little sister would come out, and I would get rid of her by telling

her that my aunt had candy for her in the trailer. Eventually I got a
whipping for lying, but it worked for a while." My friend now shares
a spacious six-room house in Berkeley with two sleepy cats and a small,
quiet watchdog.

My own privacy needs were similar. Ten years into a carefree and
princely only childhood, my parents decided they couldn't live without
seeing General Eisenhower nominated for the presidency, so they went
out and purchased a television "set" (that was what TV's were invariably
called then—as if they came in pairs). For me, the arrival of that bulky
brown box was like the arrival of a baby brother—fascinating at first,
then mildly troublesome, then downright irritating, and finally reveal-
ing itself for what it was: a ghastly and irrevocable mistake my parents
had made without consulting me.

By then we were living year round in a thirty-two-footer, just about
the longest trailer you could pull freely across any and all state lines.
The television, a seventeen-inch Admiral (big for its age in 1952) squat-
ted like an enormous toad on the Formica counter that divided the
trailer's kitchen from its living room, the counter that accordioned out
each evening to become our dinner table. The political conventions, of
course, were only an excuse, only the opening wedge of the TV invasion. Almost immediately the 6:00 news began to take precedence over
dinner conversation. A kind of gag rule was imposed, even during the
commercials (they were so new, so clever!) and family patterns of talk
a decade old melted and flowed and recongealed around the weekly
TV schedule. All three of us awoke to Dave Garroway, said good night
to Walter Winchell. On drowsy Thursday afternoons in school, without
consciously knowing what day it was, I would find myself humming
the theme song of some Thursday night TV program, so completely
did television take over the rhythm of our lives.

Almost every night, right after dinner, a neighbor or two would drop
by to see what was on, for TVs were still rare, and they attracted
neighbors in exactly the same way that, when lugged out onto the patio
at night, they attracted moths. These neighbors would park their hams
comfortably on our couch, which happened to be my bed, fold their
arms across their bellies and settle in for the evening. I came to resent
such nightly invasions of our small, private world almost as much as
I resented the box itself—that glaring, jittering eyeball with its machine-

gun yammer that dominated the household from stem to stern, ines-
capable even back in the far reaches of my parents' bedroom.

Although I'd been as captivated as everyone else at first, I quickly
began to find TV programs as boringly predictable as the commercials
that interrupted them. By age twelve I'd learned to sneak out the back
door and loosen the antenna wire, so that the first strong gust of night
wind would tear it free (no antenna, no picture) and break the collective
spell in the living room, reminding parents and neighbors alike that it
was past everybody's bedtime. This small act of subversion was satisfying out of all proportion to its importance; how little power children
have over their world!

By the late forties almost all the trailers on the better parks, the
working-class parks, were postwar models. During the war it seemed
that nearly every house trailer in America had been begged, borrowed,
or stolen by defense workers and military personnel. Thousands of
homemade jobs, and almost every factory model ever built, were
herded into makeshift camps and packed with two-, three-, and four-
child families "temporarily," until regular housing became available—
which it seldom did. A lot of these old rigs made the supreme sacrifice
and were hauled to the scrapheap soon after V-J Day. Most of the
others drifted away—to back yards and hunting leases and farmers'
chicken runs—to make room for a newer, sleeker generation of trailers.
The cardboard government rigs that survived the war were donated by
the hundreds to colleges and universities to house the GI Bill GIs who
flooded the campuses between World War II and the Korean War.

What you saw in the better parks of the late forties were a lot of
shiny new metal-clad coaches, trailers that reflected the advances—
quantum leaps, really—in aircraft technology made during the war:
riveted aluminum or steel skins, plexiglass windows, sleek futuristic
styling, lighter and stronger materials for sinks and bathtubs and
shower stalls.

Leatherette and plywood exteriors pretty much died with the war,
although masonite, curiously enough, hung on well into the fifties.
Masonite was heavy, masonite warped and buckled when moisture got
behind it, but as a trailer skin masonite had its virtues. It was certainly
tougher than either artificial leather or plywood, and it needed less

upkeep. It was cooler than metal, a better insulator, and easier for most builders to work with. From the small manufacturer's viewpoint—and most postwar trailer companies were still small—masonite was simply too cheap and paintable and low-tech to give up. Some of the best builders, some of the master craftsmen of the trailer industry, never did give it up. My family's last rig, a 1952 model designed by a respected old-time Michigan trailerman named Rex Anderson, had masonite sidewalls under a riveted aluminum roof. Many of Rex Anderson's trailers from the forties and fifties are still in use. You'll find them today in the older, shabbier, trailers-for-rent parks, still as smooth and warp-free and watertight as they were forty years ago—a tribute to both designer and masonite alike.

But the classic postwar house trailer, and the one that has outlasted all others, was the Spartan, made in Tulsa, Oklahoma by J. Paul Getty's Spartan Aircraft Corporation. Early Spartans—they first hit the market in 1946—came in two styles, Buck Rogers and caravan. The caravans, or "ham can" models, flat-sided and flat-roofed, were called "Spartanettes," as if they were the Getty team's dancing girls. Spartanettes came with aluminum skins or, for a few dollars less and a few pounds more, with masonite skins painted to imitate aluminum. Either way, the Spartanettes were the company's low-priced models, their "fighting brands."

Spartan's top-of-the-line coach—their Buck Rogers model, their futuristic spaceship-on-wheels—was called the Manor. Like the Bowlus Road Chief of 1935, like Wally Byam's Airstreams, Spartan Manors were all aircraft-riveted aluminum on the outside. Up front they were as round and sleek as a Florsheim, with a roof line that tapered aerodynamically in the rear, and if they happened to look, in silhouette, almost exactly like the Greyhound busses of the era, this was certainly not Getty's intention.

The front half of the Manor, the living room/kitchen half, was practically all window: great, swooping curves of bomber-cockpit plexiglass, neatly outlined in black rubber weatherstrip and backed by acres and acres of pure white (was there any other color?) venetian blinds. A perfectly round, opaque glass porthole hung like a full moon in the front door, and another just like it in the rear door, which was on the far side of the coach, to allay people's fears of being trapped in a trailer blown over onto its side. Both these doors were so tight, so perfectly fitted, that they shut with an airy *whoosh,* exactly like the doors on a Volkswagen Beetle.

And then there was the Spartan cabinetry—cabinetry the pickiest old stubbly faced cuss of a finish carpenter could live with. Fine-grain birch veneers, these cabinets, hand fitted and varnished to a high gloss, with every corner tongue-and-grooved together, every glue joint and every screw carefully hidden from sight. Hinges and latches were all aircraft quality chrome. Genuine formica on the counters, too—none of those cheap, rubbery linoleum countertops like the prewar trailers had. And in the living room there was "indirect lighting"—meaning fluorescent tubes hidden behind the valances of the venetian blinds, a brainstorm of those clever people who called themselves interior decorators. In the late forties, with the Curtiss Aerocars defunct for almost a decade, J. Paul Getty's Spartan Manor was just about the classiest and ruggedest and best-towing and most expensive house trailer money could buy.

After the war, nobody built their own trailer—just nobody. Between Pearl Harbor and Nagasaki, house trailer technology, always closely allied to aircraft technology, had simply spun its wheels and accelerated off into the future, leaving the back yard mechanic and basement experimenter in the dust. In 1935—even as late as 1941—a home craftsman with a modicum of skill and a few good-quality hand tools might duplicate a Traveleze or a Kozy-Coach or a Covered Wagon right down to the chassis. But only a full-scale aircraft factory could create a neatly-riveted, electrically welded, plexiglass-windowed Spartan Manor. After the war, virtually everyone who wanted a house trailer stood in line for a factory model. And because only twenty or thirty companies had survived the war, the choice of new models was at first limited.

This gave the postwar parks an air of uniformity, of conformity, that had been missing in the pioneer decade, when one out of every three trailers was likely to be a one-of-a-kind home-built, the other two coming from any one of over seven hundred commercial builders. This early hodgepodge of shape and size and style suited perfectly the temperament of the prewar—the pioneer—trailerite.

But after the war people didn't seem to mind the idea of uniformity. After the war, trailerites became a lot less interested in customizing their rigs, a lot less likely to take saw in hand to reshape a trailer interior to individual whims, putting a magazine rack here, an extra cupboard there, a bigger window over the kitchen table, the way prewar trailerites had done. Perhaps four years of war had tempered the trailerites' spirit of rebelliousness and individuality. Perhaps four years of rationing and material shortages had made mass-produced uniformity—the so-called "economies of scale"—more acceptable to them. (Outside the parks, during this same period, Levittowns were booming.) For whatever reason, it was OK, after the war, if my Spartan, or Alma, or National, looked exactly like yours. After all, your rig's in space 28, and mine's in 32. Or is that my rig in 28 and the Johnson's in 32 and yours over in . . . say, what color's your awning, anyway?

The pioneer models that survived the war, the little 1930s leatherette and plywood boxes, were gathered onto small, decrepit parks during the late forties and turned into low-dollar rentals, and almost overnight a new kind of slum landlord was born. These were the sad little parks of everyone's memory, poorly lighted, poorly drained, never paved and seldom grassy, full of solitary elderly folk trying to hold onto their health and independence with a monthly pittance from Social Security: brave, lonely souls without family or friends, forgotten people from another war, another century, a generation whose fires were flickering low.

Here too were the abandoned families: thin, tired mothers and a ragged kid or two, or more, eking out a living by taking in washing and sewing, by giving piano lessons on a miniature spinet in a miniature living room. These were people no poorer, on the whole, than the invisible folk stacked twenty high in the brick slums of inner cities, and the trailerite poor, at least, had access in good weather to sunshine and fresh air. But winter would come and find these little households without a car to hitch up to, without tires for the trailer, even. And how do you stay warm in a bedroom while the north wind is nuzzling all six of its sides?

Such trailer slums were, all too often, even more visible than conventional slums, for the simple reason that they weren't gathered into one easily avoidable section of town. They might pop up unexpectedly along almost any suburban thoroughfare, sprawling out behind a hand-lettered sign that said TRAILERS FOR RENT BY DAY OR WEEK. The image of poverty that dogged middle-class trailerites throughout the quarter-century or so of their existence was never more fully realized than in these postwar slum parks, where even some of the government's sad old cardboard trailers of 1942–43 came finally to rest.

And so postwar prosperity accelerated a trend that had already begun on the parks in the late thirties—a trend towards two distinct economic classes within the trailerite subculture. Call them the haves and the have-nots, say they came either from the "better" parks or the "rental" parks—however you label the two groups, they represented a widening gap in the blue-collar world of the trailerite, a gap that had been only just visible back in the days of the tin can tourists and their "great wheeled democracy"—back in the depression-ridden thirties when your friends were my friends and my friends were yours. By the late forties that gregarious, egalitarian world of 1936 must have seemed as far off as Job's land of Uz—as far off as it seems today.

World War II was in some ways a watershed in American culture fully as significant as World War I. To look back on the thirties with postwar eyes is to see a nation that was, to a great extent, homogenous in its poverty. The gap between the middle class and the poor was much narrower then, and much more likely to be bridged by empathy than it is today. In the thirties, most Americans who were able to eat regularly (and there's no better definition of "middle class") had missed a meal or two in the past—or at least knew people who had. In those days almost every neighborhood had its hardscrabble families, but they weren't considered alien, simply poor. For poverty, even in the Great Depression, was still a circumstance; it had not yet come to be thought of as a distinct subculture. The poor we had always with us, but we still presumed them to share most of our ideals and aspirations. We didn't yet have the leisure, or the distance, to begin seeing them as different.

This attitude began to change after the war, as a new wave of working-class prosperity swept the country, widening the gap between the haves and the have-nots, between the people who missed meals and the people who didn't. And the trailer parks, those unconsulted barometers of American culture, were quick to register this change. The old prewar gradation from front to rear, from gold coaster to sage

"The permanent trailer camp offers all the bad features of the urban 'blighted area,' none of the vacation adventure for which trailers were made."
—"Trailer Camp Slums," *The Survey*, October 1951

brusher, became less and less satisfactory to the image-conscious, upwardly mobile trailerites of the later forties. As newer parks opened
up, they gravitated to them, leaving the poor folk in their prewar rigs
behind, much as the urban middle class, in their flight to the suburbs,
were abandoning the inner city to the poor.

To a growing number of this still-growing subculture, the park
where they lived, and its appearance, was becoming increasingly important. Most of the prewar trailerites, those tin can tourists and
middle-aged rebels who had founded the trailer life, cared little for
appearances: if their camp irritated a few passers-by, a few sticks-in-
the-mud, well, so much the better. But the postwar trailerite felt little
of this cantankerous defiance, this typically thirties rebelliousness
against "the system." For after all, times were good: the system had not
failed them as it had the pioneers. Also, they were becoming less inclined to think of themselves as tourists, mere passers-through. Despite
better tires and better roads and better towcars, the trailerites of the
late forties and early fifties were beginning to stay longer in one place
than the pioneers had. They were beginning to talk more of settling
down, of finding a place that suited them and "putting down some
roots."

> "Shirt-sleeved trailer
> dwellers tilted back in
> their chairs glaring right
> back at the high-hat
> neighbors who live in
> swank apartment houses
> just across the street."
> —*The New York Times,*
> September 19, 1937

"We have tried to avoid thinking about trailers, and about the way
Americans are losing their roots," wrote an anonymous staffer at *The
New Yorker* in November of 1936, when the American trailer movement
was just getting under way. Four months later *Fortune* picked up the
refrain, calling the country's quarter-million trailerites "rootless as air
plants." Then *The New York Times* chimed in, "Trailer folk who follow
the sun north and south with the seasons are kin to the pioneers who
never could sink permanent roots." And so "rootlessness" became one
more in the long list of public charges against the trailer subculture.
The image dogged them throughout the quarter-century of their existence: trailerites were floaters, drifters, people without cultural or economic ties to the region where they lived, people without roots.

Roots. It's an amusing concept, if you think about it: a vegetable
metaphor applied to members of the animal kingdom, as if we were
all turnips rather than human beings. It's especially amusing when
wielded by some anonymous thirties scribbler at the *Times* or the *New*

Yorker, a person who by all odds was a transplanted midwesterner, sleeping each night in a rent-controlled cubicle twenty stories up in the air over Manhattan. Roots, indeed.

When I think of the people I've known with roots—the true vegetable people—I think first of Jesse, my father's older brother, who inherited the family farm. Uncle Jess might be said to have been rooted, at least by American standards: he was the fifth generation born on that particular piece of Ohio farmland since it was settled, around 1800. Is a hundred years in the same place sufficient to establish roots? Then how about fifty? Twenty-five? Ten, maybe? And by whose standards? Best ask a Californian, one of those hydroponic folk who currently changes addresses every three years, and not, say, a Scot from the Isle of Skye.

With all due respect to Arthur Haley, who popularized the term, it seems more useful to think of Americans not in terms of their roots but their dotted lines—the imaginary trail they've left in arriving where they are now. My grandfather, for example, was a farmer and a carpenter who lived all his life on the same half-section of land; his dotted line was reasonably simple. My father's, especially after his marriage to my mother, became more complex. And my own, even omitting the trailer years of childhood, seems incredibly convoluted: thirteen addresses on two continents in twenty-four years of marriage. These numbers surprise even me, and yet they're not atypical of postwar America, where people—upwardly, downwardly, laterally mobile—bounce about with Brownian motion. I presently live near a city of half a million people, and I can't name a dozen adult acquaintances who were born here.

So, for an American at least, certainly for a westerner, "Tell me about your dotted line" probably makes more sense than "Tell me about your roots." And the trailerites—weather-wise, street-wise, tax-wise, always on the move, yet always on the lookout for that ideal place to settle down—had begun stretching and looping and twisting and *making interesting* their dotted line even before the rest of America did. They did this well before the war; they did this during the war, and they continued for perhaps half a dozen years afterward.

> "May you live in interesting times."
> —Chinese toast

And then, almost abruptly, they stopped.

It happened in the early fifties, the Sinatra years. The Good War

was over, Korea was winding down, and all the boiling, bubbling turbulence of Truman and Joe McCarthy was finally beginning to thicken
and congeal into the strawberry Jello era of Ike and Mamie. By this
time, two million, maybe two and a half million Americans were living
on wheels, and they, too, could feel the atmosphere thickening around
them. Every year it seemed to get a little harder to move, a little easier
to find excuses for staying put: the kids are doing well in school, we
really like this park, found a church that made us welcome, best fishing
in America, not a bad climate, this new rig's so blamed heavy and hard
to pull. During the early fifties, as if on command, two million people
suddenly began to lose their wanderlust, began giving up their seasonal
gadding, their perennial search for utopia, and started settling into the
parks like gulls on a nesting ground.

> "Trailerites have become
> sluggish. A recent survey
> showed that the typical
> trailer coach is moved
> only once a year. The av-
> erage move is 200 miles."
> —*Popular Science
> Monthly,* June 1954

A survey taken as early as 1951 by the Trailer Coach Manufacturers
Association found that the average trailerite was staying put for over
twenty months at a time. "Average" is an amusing word, when applied
to people rather than numbers—but it basically meant that, to balance
the "snow birds" like my parents (who moved at least twice a year just
to follow the sun, and sometimes once or twice in between to get away
from neighbors who kept a barking dog or cooked with too much
garlic or spoke approvingly of Adlai Stevenson), a larger and larger
number of trailerites were beginning to stay put for years at a time.
Fortune, a magazine that never made any pretense of understanding the
trailerite mentality, read these statistics and shook its editorial head in
wonder:

> There is nothing in the [TCMA] survey, however, that indicates why
> [so many] American families who have enough money to buy a house
> and lot buy a house and wheels instead, and then elect to move about
> as little as possible.

James Jones, who wrote *From Here to Eternity* in the living room of
his twenty-six-foot Spartan, understood both aspects of trailering, the
lure of park life as well as the song of the open road:

> I had a bath in mine, but I preferred to go over to the wash house for
> my shower anyway, and listen to the conversation of the men and boys
> as they shaved or washed up after work. . . . Many of them have settled
> into permanent jobs in a town and just gone on living in trailers anyway;

By 1950, with trailers getting bigger and heavier, trailerites were beginning to stay put longer between moves. The trailer era was passing and the beginning of the mobile home era was at hand.

I suspect it gives them a feeling they can always quit and move on, even though they know they may never do it.

"We can be outa here by noon"—that phrase that should have hung, in cross-stitch, in every trailer living room, was fading from memory, losing its galvanic appeal. The generation of idealists and crusty iconoclasts who had founded the trailer movement back in the thirties was passing, and in its place was a younger and more pragmatic generation, a generation still attracted by the warmth and informality of the parks, by the old tin can tourist spirit of neighborliness and cooperation—

but increasingly seduced by the siren song of status and upward mobility, by the huckster's constant insinuation that a person can somehow rise above himself, and his neighbors, by climbing a pile of possessions.

And how could this postwar generation have been otherwise? For the second Great Age of Gadgetry was sweeping America, and it made the first gadget era—the 1920s—seem unimaginative by comparison. After the war, TVs and record players and garbage disposals and air-conditioners fell from the skies like hailstones, rained down to fill the dreams and empty the pockets of the whole GI generation. And this rain of material goods fell impartially, upon householder and trailerite alike. But where, oh Lord, was the trailer dweller to put all this marvelous new gadgetry? Responding to this pressure, the postwar trailers—themselves a part of the rain of consumer goods—had already begun to grow longer. Now, quite suddenly, they sailed right over the magic thirty-three-foot line, the maximum allowable length for permit-free towing. Now they sprawled to forty, forty-five, fifty feet—too long to move, too long even to sit still for any length of time without jacks under the body, lest they sag on both ends like a stick of licorice candy.

The world had at last caught up with the trailerites; they were no longer safely ahead of time. In fact, because of their limited space, they were beginning to feel behind the times, instead. There was too little room in their living rooms for TVs and hi-fi's and lounge chairs and hutches; too little room in the kitchens for electric mixers and broilers and dishwashers and toaster ovens; too little room in the bathrooms for heat lamps and weight scales and hair dryers and four kinds of shampoo. Their castles were simply too small to remain "modern." Like the dinosaurs at the close of the Cretaceous, the world they had adapted to so marvelously had finally moved on, passing them by. The hour of extinction was at hand.

The man who stepped in to oversee this extinction was a trailer builder himself, a farm boy named Elmer William John Frey, of Marshfield, Wisconsin. Frey, an ex-carnival worker, ex-electrician, ex-musician, marched home to Marshfield right after World War II and decided to apply his diverse talents to the building of homes on wheels. He rounded up most of his available family—three younger brothers, one

"For full-time living purposes no trailer is too big."
—*Westways,* April 1950

"This television business has emphasized the almost universal desire of home trailerites for a large living room."
—John Gartner,
All about Trailers, 1954

brother-in-law, and an uncle—and created, out in the family barn, a company he called "Rollohome, Inc." The year was 1946.

Family businesses being what they are, the six of them managed to assemble only one complete trailer before the year expired. By the time it sold, they had 1,200 man-hours in it, almost ten times the industry average. But they soon got their collective acts together, and by 1952 Rollohome had become an industry leader turning out thirty-five units a week—eight-wides, of course, because in 1952 that's all the law allowed, in every one of the forty-eight states.

Frey had long thought this law outmoded. Modern trailers (he insisted, quite rightly, on calling them mobile homes, even fancied he had invented the phrase) needed to be not only longer, but wider. People wanted more room. People *deserved* more room. You bet, his family said, and the people in hell want ice water, too. The law of the land says eight feet max. What do you plan to do about that, Elmer?

Change the law, Frey replied. And, almost single-handedly, he did.

Early in 1954, Elmer Frey sold his interest in Rollohome and used the money to found Marshfield Homes, a company dedicated to building nothing but ten-foot-wide coaches—vehicles that were illegal on every highway in America. He got around the laws by shipping his overwide models to the trailer shows on railroad flatcars. And at every show, customers simply went wild for them. He started pointing this out to state legislatures all across the country, in person, at his own expense: people wanted ten-wides.

Trailerites, Frey maintained, weren't trailering much any more; they were settling down. What they needed was living space, not mobility. These new, wider coaches that he was proposing, these mobile homes, wouldn't be a nuisance on the highway because they'd be on the highway only once, moving from factory to park. He showed the legislators statistics, and they were true statistics: the bigger the house trailer, the less often it moved. If people wanted to travel, Frey argued, they'd get themselves a travel trailer, one of those little aluminum things built out in Los Angeles, and park it out beside their house, or mobile home, to go vacationing in.

Elmer Frey was right, of course, and for once, right prevailed. Suddenly, almost magically, the maximum-width laws began to crumble: first in Arizona, in '55; then, later in that same year, in Frey's home

state of Wisconsin. One by one, the rest of the states came around—
and so did the rest of the trailer builders. By the end of the decade,
the eight-wide coach was finished: except in travel trailer size, you
could hardly give one away. By the time John Kennedy came to power,
by the time the rest of America began to break its long sleep, began
casting off its postwar lethargy and starting to move again, the trailerites, always out of step, were settling down.

People who still lived in an old-fashioned eight-wide set one foot in
their neighbor's new "ten," and something snapped in their brains.
Instantly they knew that they never wanted to go back to their claustrophobic little broom closet again. Instantly they were ready to trade
their freedom of the road—they weren't using it anyway—for those
two extra feet of elbow room. Overnight, two decades of postwar trailers became hand-me-downs, closeouts, make-me-an-offer specials that
were quickly relegated to the hardscrabble parks, the trailers-for-rent
parks, where many of them remain today.

Overnight, an entire way of life came to an end. Parks remodeled,
widening and deepening their lots to accommodate the new models—
and raising their rents accordingly. Tens-wides, twelve-wides, then
double-wides (two eights that joined to make a sixteen) each became,
successively, the norm. And each new model got longer, and flashier,
and flimsier, for now they didn't have to be built to stand the rigors
of the highway: two or three moves, at most, would cover a mobile
home's lifetime. As their wheels shrank in symbolic value, they began
to shrink in size as well. Trailer wheels had been larger and heavier
than those of the towcar; mobile home wheels shriveled to the size of
chocolate doughnuts. Wheels ceased to be an integral part of the
coach—now they were simply another element in the delivery system.
Like the hitch, and the diesel bobtail, and the diesel bobtail's anonymous driver, the wheels were just one of the accessories needed to
move the unit from builder to buyer. As soon as a mobile home was
sited, wheels and hitch went back to the factory for credit—exactly as
in the cardboard trailer days of World War II.

The public at large continued to call these monsters trailers, much
to the chagrin of builder and buyer alike. But they weren't trailers,
hadn't really been trailers since they crossed the thirty-three-foot line,
back in the early fifties. The Age of the Mobile Home—which William

BING CROSBY TO OPEN HALF-
MILLION-DOLLAR PARK IN
PALM SPRINGS
—headline, *Trailer Life*,
October 1954

Stout had foreseen, and named, in 1936—had finally arrived. And the old house trailer, with its air of carefree living, its ability to follow the sun, or work, or rumors of work, back and forth across America on an hour's notice, simply was no more.

12 Interred with their Bones

Except for tire replacement, there is virtually nothing to wear out in one of these modern trailers.

—Popular Mechanics,
December 1936

Take nothing but photographs; leave nothing but footprints.

—*national park slogan*

The Merle Norman Classic Beauty Collection, a privately-owned museum in the San Fernando Valley, numbers among its treasures a 1937 Pierce Arrow twelve-cylinder limousine. Hitched to the big limo's rear bumper is yet another Pierce-Arrow, also 1937 vintage: one of the few remaining Travelodge Model As, a nineteen-foot, aluminum-clad camping trailer. The museum exhibits car and trailer with a full regalia of picnic dishes and Thermos jugs, all ready for a carefree weekend in Yosemite.

Salvaged from a farmer's hen yard, the little Travelodge has been lovingly restored: fresh birch plywood on interior walls and ceiling, reproduction red gumwood cabinetry, authentic lavatory and toilet perched inside a miniature showerstall-*cum*-bathroom where generations of chickens once nested. The trailer's eighteen-gauge aluminum skin, which protected it from the elements for half a century and is virtually the only reason the coach remained intact for restoration, is painted the same deep and glorious blue as the limousine up front. Together, limo and trailer present a sleek and elegant image of wealth and leisure in the faraway thirties—sleek and elegant, and almost totally false.

176

Of the four-hundred-odd Travelodges built during the Pierce-Arrow Corporation's deathbed romance with the house trailer, probably fewer than a dozen were ever hitched to a Pierce-Arrow automobile for anything but publicity purposes. The vast majority of the Travelodges, like the vast majority of the other moderately priced camping trailers of the era, were sold to trailerites—full-timers—and not to wealthy vacationists who went motoring about the countryside in twelve-cylinder limousines.

The image of trailer-as-toy, which the manufacturers went to so much trouble to plant in the public mind during the thirties, still persists, and a good thing it does, too, for without it, who would have saved any of the old rigs? Henry Ford's Model T, the poor man's automobile, has been restored, rejuvenated, reproduced by the thousands. But the house trailer, home to five million blue-collar Americans between 1935 and 1960, has been tossed aside, forgotten, relegated to the national garbage heap along with all the other bright and fragile boxes that our dreams come in.

The Merle Norman Travelodge and handful of other early trailers that have escaped oblivion owe their good fortune to the belief that they were once some rich person's plaything. To point out that the little blue Travelodge was, for most of its active lifetime, almost certainly somebody's home, that long before it became a hen house, cotton-diapered babies crawled the linoleum of that six-by-eight living room, learned to walk by pulling themselves up on the nickel-plated handles of those hand finished gumwood cabinets, slept away their childhoods on that clever "gaucho" davenport, would be to devalue the vehicle in almost everyone's eyes. The museum makes no secret of the fact that the Travelodge once housed chickens, but nowhere does it mention the human beings, the "trailer trash," who clucked over the little coach in its heyday, who came home to roost in it every night.

Pierce-Arrow was only one of some eight hundred to two thousand house trailer manufacturers who plied their trade before the World War II. Where is their handiwork today? The next time you visit a museum of history or transportation, ask to see an old trailer, ask to see just one of the homes of those million Americans who battled the Great Depression on wheels, those economic guerillas of the thirties who took to the streets and highways in their struggle for survival. All you'll get is a blank stare. There are more nineteenth-century sheep-

"The majority of trailers are pulled by Chevrolets, Fords, and Plymouths."
—*Harper's*, March 1937

Sarasota, Florida, 1941. A retired couple relaxes in front of their Pierce-Arrow Travelodge. Because prewar trailers were so small, people today think of them as campers, yet seventy-five to ninety percent of them were full-time homes.

herder wagons than twentieth-century house trailers preserved among our national collectibles. Why? Because the old Basque sheepherder, with his eight words of English, his bilingual collie, and his unobstructed view of five hundred square miles of Wyoming, is a romantic figure in our mythology, but that indigenous American gypsy, the trailerite, is not. And museum directors, even more than the rest of us, are suckers for romance.

The early "coach" or "bread-loaf" trailers, still common a quarter-century ago, are now almost extinct. You can count the museum models on one hand. The Henry Ford Museum in Dearborn owns a much modified Stage Coach, a twenty-three-footer built in northern Indiana during the mid-thirties. This particular trailer derives most of its charisma from having been used by Charles and Anne Morrow Lindbergh during the forties and fifties as a travel trailer and back yard retreat: Anne Morrow Lindbergh logged every trip they took on the bottom of one of the kitchen drawers. And the Auburn-Cord-Dusenberg Museum in Auburn, Indiana, has on loan a Covered Wagon right out of Arthur Sherman's heyday: a 1935 Master model, with oak chassis, two-tone leatherette sidewalls, and wire-spoke wheels—a genuine classic among early bread-loafs, and just possibly the sole remaining example of what was once the most popular trailer in America.

"Oh, those Covered Wagons were everywhere!"
—Ruth Bowlus, in conversation, 1988

The manufacturers have done little better in preserving their past than the museums. Only three of the prewar builders are still in business. One, Airstream, owns a 1937 Clipper, one of founder Wally Byam's earliest all-aluminum coaches. Affectionately dubbed "Old Grandad," the Clipper looks, at a glance, surprisingly like a modern Airstream; only its small windows and ultrastreamlined roostertail betray its Buck Rogers era vintage. Old Grandad is on permanent display at the company plant in Jackson Center, Ohio. Occasionally one of its contemporaries shows up at a Wally Byam Caravan Club rally, the pride of some private collector.

The other two prewar builders are Schult Homes, which began life in Elkhart, Indiana, and Redman Homes, originally of Alma, Michigan. Both dropped the word "trailer" from their names thirty or more years ago; today their products are known as "manufactured housing," the latest euphemism for the mobile home. Schult, now in Middlebury, Indiana, owns one restored early model, a 1940 Nomad, eighteen feet long, a leatherette and canvas breadloaf similar to the one my parents were living in when I was born. Texas-based Redman won't answer letters about its past. The company got its start in 1937 building blatant imitations of the popular Alma Silvermoon, a masonite ham can with a distinctive, upswept duck-tail in the rear that was intended, so the story went, to prevent the bumper from dragging when going over curbs.

A fourth pioneer manufacturer, Trotwood Trailers, of Trotwood, Ohio, burned in the early eighties, destroying all three pioneer coaches

in its collection, including a Kozy-Coach built up in Kalamazoo as well
as a classic caravan-style Trotwood Ranger.

Not surprisingly, the only trailer America has preserved in any number is the gaudy, impractical Curtiss Aerocar—the trailer with the
golden halo. Unlike the Travelodge or the Covered Wagon or the early
Airstreams, Glenn Curtiss's luxurious Aerocar Land Yachts actually ful-
filled the toy myth so dear to the pioneer trailerman's heart: very few
of them ever became anyone's home.

More image than substance, the typical Aerocar had little to offer
the full-time trailer dweller. It was as long and narrow and as full of
windows as a bus—one of the few trailers intended to be occupied
while in motion rather than at rest. Its patented "Aerocoupler" fifth-
wheel hitch was designed around an honest-to-goodness fifth wheel: a
small aircraft tire mounted in the towcar's rumble seat. The Aerocoupler
cushioned the trailer's ride marvelously, although it proved to be just
as susceptible to flats as any other 1930s tire.

Curtiss created the Aerocar as a luxury commuter vehicle, a traveling
stateroom, a highway version of the private Pullman car rather than a
mere camping or living device. And he priced it accordingly. A few
"fleet" models, custom-built display vans for large corporations like
RCA and Singer Sewing Machine, fell into private hands and were
converted to house trailers. But most Aerocars and their imitators
tended to be strictly playtoys for the rich, as far beyond the reach of
the average thirties trailerite as a quarter-million-dollar motor home is
for a blue-collar laborer today.

Oilman H. L. Doherty, president of Cities Service, once owned not
one but two of these showboats—a matched pair of thirty-seven-foot-
ers. He kept them coupled to a pair of spiffy, chauffeur-driven Reo
coupes and used them in a private game of leapfrog between New York
and Miami. While the millionaire and a few select traveling companions
rolled along in airconditioned comfort in the number one vehicle—
toying, perhaps, with compass and altimeter, ordering hors d'oeuvres
from their onboard chef, taking turns showering in the tiled bathroom—the number two would speed ahead with a galley full of servants busily at work on the noon meal. At some prearranged stop,
Doherty and company would troop over to the already parked number

"We only had one flat on
that Curtiss hitch, but it
took us half a day to jack
the trailer up high enough
to unhitch, so we could
patch it."
—former trailerite
Mrs. Floyd McIver of
Detroit, Michigan,
in conversation, 1989

two, dine on white linen, and then leisurely return to their coach for the afternoon ride. Sometime before sundown they would be passed discreetly by their dining car, rushing ahead with the evening meal. At night, servants and chauffeurs would bed down in number two, beside whatever swank hotel the intrepid travelers had chosen for the night.

This was a favorite story among trailer salesmen before the war. Nevertheless, it was not what was commonly implied, during the pioneer era, by the phrase "trailer life."

What has become of the million and a half to two million house trailers that rolled off factory assembly lines, or took shape in garages and barns and cabinet shops, during the turbulent quarter-century of the trailerite era? Most of the shiny, metallic postwar models, the "tin boxes" of the forties and fifties, are still with us. Some have become portable office space for used-car lots and Christmas tree bazaars and a hundred other ephemeral small businesses. Some have been turned into rolling toolsheds and field offices for construction companies. Some are vacation cabins; others have sprouted pontoons to become houseboats on lakes and rivers. Thousands are still homes—scattered across rural America, on farms and ranches, along muddy backwoods lanes, in almost any area where the housing codes are lax and the neighbors unpretentious.

But the majority of these postwar rigs, square-cornered eight-wides from the long, long trailer era, are to be found in the older, trailers-for-rent parks around the fringes of almost every town and city. Like most rental property, they look conspicuously unloved. On most of them, the hitches and wheels remain ironically intact, the relics of a bygone era; it's obvious they're not going anywhere.

An occasional round-roofed masonite model nestles among them, looking like a ghost from the thirties. Is it really a prewar? Probably not. A lot of masonite coaches were built during 1945 and 1946, using prewar jigs and patterns, just as 1946 auto builders used prewar stamps and dies for some of their models. The trailer spotter's rule of thumb says: if the coach is watertight and habitable, it was probably built after World War II. Still, it's worth a look, worth an inquiry. After all, hundreds of masonite-covered Alma Silvermoons, bought by the Farm

"In the year 2000 a.d. many of today's Spartans will still be in daily use."
—Spartan Trailercoach ad, *Trailer Life,* September 1948

Security Administration during the "emergency" of 1940–41, have survived nearly half a century of brutal, high-country winters out on the
Navajo and Hopi reservations of northern Arizona, and are still in use.

Most of the little bread-loaf models built before the war, with their
canvas over plywood roofs and soft leatherette sidewalls, have simply
melted away. The plains and deserts are littered with their skeletons:
tall wooden ribs that stand up like the inverted hulls of old sailing
ships—easy to pick out, after you've seen one or two, though sometimes difficult to identify by maker. More numerous, but harder to
spot, are the prewar home-builts, squat and shacklike and all too easily
dismissed as just another old hen coop or toolshed. Push aside the
weeds around the bottom and there's a wheel well, an axle, a rusty
hitch with the barely visible legend: Zagelmeyer AutoCamp, Bay City,
Mich. Only hints and outlines of the thirties trailers remain.

Metal-clads like the Merle Norman Travelodge were relatively rare
before the war. Out in Los Angeles, Bowlus and Airstream each built
a handful of their aluminum jellybeans, and a firm in Alhambra known
as the Hollywood Steel Trailer Company turned out a small number
of bus-shaped coaches called the Hollywood Nomad. Firms in Chicago
produced a hopelessly ugly metal bread-loaf, the Land Cruiser, and a
unique, round-nosed, turret-roofed model, all glass and steel, called
the Stream-Lite. Hayes Body, in Grand Rapids, built hundreds of steel
imitations of the Covered Wagon, and Sherman himself, starting in
November of 1936, offered his trailers in "Shermanite steel," a thin
sheet of metal bonded to plywood.

Where are these metal-clads today? The aluminum and steel trailers
of the Great Depression have disappeared, melted down, right along
with the the canvas and leatherette models. Most metal trailers of that
era still had canvas roofs, and once a trailer roof begins to leak, moisture
seeps in to attack the thin veneer on walls and ceiling, and the entire
structure begins very quickly to sag and warp and come apart like a
wet cigar box.

Occasionally some travel trailer dealer will restore an old coach and
keep it about for a conversation piece. But these tend to be postwar
models like the Airstream and Silver Streak—small, sleek, all-aluminum rigs built primarily for vacationing rather than living, built to
sit out in the weather unused and unloved for months at a time, trailers

meant to be treated as toys, not homes. The tedious, fragile, early biplane construction of the typical prewar coach seems to have little appeal for restorers and collectors, and of course the low-life image of the inexpensive wood and canvas trailer adds nothing to its collectibility. Most of the pioneer trailers—like the trailerites themselves— have been swept under the rich tapestry of history's rug.

Something like a million Americans lived on wheels before the war, and another three or four million joined the movement between Pearl Harbor and the close of the era, in the fifties. Many of these ex-trailerites are baby boomers, born and raised in the parks just as I was. And most of them have put the experience out of mind, just as I had. Until a couple of years ago, when an old coach in a vacant lot jogged my memory, I hadn't thought seriously about my trailer days, my life in the parks, for almost thirty years.

What made me forget such a significant aspect of my childhood? Was it simple snobbery, a covert embarrassment? In interviewing former trailerites, I've noticed a curious correlation between educational level and memory: the more schooling people have, the harder it is for them to recall their trailer life. High school drop-outs from rural Kansas cheerfully recount tales of elopement in homemade trailers pulled by battered "hoopies" (a regional term of endearment for any decrepit automobile). But give a person a year or two of college and it can take an hour of prodding to uncover the memory of once having lived, however briefly, in one of these little galloping bungalows.

As a child, I was friendly and outgoing and confident, and I can't consciously recall a single incident of the sort of blatant discrimination that so many trailerites reported at the time. Nevertheless, I still managed to repress, for almost a third of a century, all thought of those dozen or more kaleidoscopic years I spent in the parks. Where did I learn this strange forgetfulness? As a child or as an adult? At school or at college? In the parks or off? The worm of prejudice can bore from within or without.

After its brief period of beatification in the mid-thirties, the American house trailer quickly sank into ignominy, becoming the symbol of poverty and ignorance, the butt of a thousand jokes. And the mobile home, the house trailer's sprawling, earth-bound successor, inherited this social stigma almost intact. Every bright young European film-

"The more there were, the fewer there are."
—saying among book collectors

"The children of the men and women who live in East Hartford's migrant trailer camp know already the sting of snobbish contempt. Their schoolmates call them 'trailer trash.'"
—*Harper's*, October 1941

maker, come over to do the obligatory anti-American satire, jumps off the plane and heads straight for the nearest mobile home park. To live in a mobile home today, even though you own not only the structure but the land beneath it, is still to be persona non grata, a second-class citizen, in caste somewhere between apartment dweller and street person. So deep and irrational is our tangled sense of "home."

But beyond snobbery, beyond class, lies an even more tangible reason for the apparent amnesia I keep encountering among former trailerites: if you were a child of the parks, you simply can't go home again, because almost all of the old parks are gone without a trace. The Alabama sharecroppers of *Let Us Now Praise Famous Men* can still visit the tumbledown cabins of their childhood, but the trailer folk of that same era have nothing but photographs to reminisce over. Perhaps no other twentieth-century style of life has disappeared so completely as that of the American trailerite.

Why? Because few modern people—and no people in history prided themselves more on being "modern"—have lived as lightly on the earth as the trailerites. Their parks consisted of a few streets, often unpaved, a clapboard washhouse or two, and a minimal water-sewage-electric grid to each lot. Most of these parks—and there were some fifteen to twenty thousand of them, by the mid-fifties—were scattered about the raw edges of cities and towns that were even then creeping outward, sprawling urban centers that have long since gobbled them up, paved them over, and forgotten them. Most of the parks that remain from the trailerite era, 1935–60, have either flowered into fancy mobile home ranches with swimming pools and putting greens and a uniformed guard at the gate, or else degenerated into slum parks full of scruffy and poorly maintained eight- and ten-wide rental units, available by the week. Both fill an obvious need in America's housing spectrum, but neither have much in common with the old-time trailer park, full of friendly, casual, but proud and independent folk who went about in shirt-sleeves and hair curlers, reminding one other with a wink not to let their hitch get rusty.

"The most pretentious camp [in Detroit] is at Gratiot and Connor Avenues, within five miles of downtown."
—*The New York Times,* June 6, 1937

What is interesting about any society, large or small, is not so much how it appears from the outside—how the world sees it—as how it appears from within, how its own members view themselves. A carnival

comes to town with its brawny and unshaven roustabouts, its hard-
eyed pitchmen and its sideshow freaks, and we suppress a shudder as
we herd our children down the midway. Who inhabits this weird,
anachronistic world? What kind of alien flesh can these people be?

We're outsiders, so we'll never know. And yet it would be worth
while to hear the stories that carny folk tell one another around their
dinner tables in the quiet, dust-settling hour after the midway closes.
It would be interesting, and probably surprising, too, to know the
myths these strangers live by, the romantic tints that their private sun
casts over the tedium and technology of their daily lives.

The term "trailerite" no doubt covered a far broader spectrum of
people than I have managed, in these few pages, to suggest: people
who would have seemed as alien to my parents and me as we must
have seemed to the Saturday night drivers who roared past the three
of us, bedded down in our little Schult beside some highway and
reading Tugboat Annie stories aloud from *The Saturday Evening Post* by
candlelight, halfway between Cincinnati and New Orleans, halfway
between Friday's world and Monday's.

Probably there were many more trailerites at the lower end of the
economic scale than I have accounted for—folk who seldom or never
dropped anchor in a trailer park, lone families who "dry camped" for
weeks and months and years behind billboards, in vacant fields, in the
back yards of relatives and friends and well-disposed strangers. I hav-
en't mentioned, because I know so little about, the thousands of Je-
hovah's Witnesses, whose stern religion demanded of each of them
three hours a day as a "Bible educator," a fiat that kept the devout
constantly on the move, often in rolling homes. Of the 100,000 Witnesses who attended the sect's 1950 New York convention, one in seven
arrived by trailer, forming a theocratic trailer city of some 2,600 rigs,
where the house-bound could follow the convention proceedings over
loudspeakers strung throughout the camp.

Nor have I attempted to paint those people who sunbathed on the
grass and frequented the private casino at the Ollie Trout Camp down
in Miami. Throughout the thirties, Ollie Trout presided over the most
extravagantly overpriced trailer park in the entire United States: "a
parking lot for Aerocars," people called it, with a mixture of jealousy
and derision in their voices. Ollie Trout's minimum rent was five dollars

a week, almost four times the going rate of other Florida parks, and from there it went straight up into that layer of the ozone commonly labeled what the market will bear. Rumor had it that the really choice lots rented for as much as twenty dollars; you could almost stay downtown at the Fontainebleau for that kind of money. But Ollie Trout had grass, acres of grass, and hibiscus bushes beyond number, and a palm tree at the corner of each lot. He had spiffy neon lights that reflected off the swaying palm fronds all night, and enough lawn chairs for every guest in camp to sit down at once. At Ollie Trout's there was an outdoor playground full of swings and slides for the little kids, and an indoor playground full of slot machines for the bigger ones. Just about everybody agreed: Ollie Trout's had *ambiance*.

The Tin Can Tourists of the World never seriously considered Ollie Trout's as a convention site. The sturdy old rank and file would have refused, merely on principle, of course, to pay his prices. Still, there was hardly a canner who didn't know Ollie Trout's name. While other trailer landlords were thumbing their thesaurus for high-toned synonyms—park, court, terrace, haven, lodge, village—Ollie Trout insisted on calling his place a camp: the Ollie Trout Camp. You could tell by his sky blue trousers (a *Fortune* reporter was sufficiently offended to label him "gorgeous") that Ollie Trout flat didn't give a damn. And although the canners may not have approved of his slot machines or his cigars or his language—the TCT had unwritten prohibitions against smoking, drinking, swearing and gambling—they nevertheless admired his spirit. It was that same defiant spirit that had brought the canners together in the first place, the same spirit that made them cling so doggedly to their own homely name.

I have not tried to paint these people, these ultimate gold coasters of the Ollie Trout Camp, because they were, for the most part, vacationers rather than full-timers. A few really did arrive in Aerocars, and some of the Aerocars really did have servants' quarters. These people were not in H. L. Doherty's class; and yet many of them were extremely wealthy, compared to the average trailerite. And money in extremes, whether too much or too little, has a way of separating us. The patrons of the Ollie Trout Camp were as far from the trailerite mainstream as was the solitary fruit tramp down along the river in his homemade rig.

And yet all of these people, the gold coasters and the fruit tramps and the broad mainstream of trailerites as well, shared a common myth. Like all good and serviceable myths, it was vague of outline and soft of color. It was faintly golden, I think, the color of the light that escaped, evenings, through the screened doors and windows of a hundred trailers nestling together under the trees, honey-colored beams from the honey-colored wood that lined these little magic lantern homes. It was a golden, an almost childishly simple, myth that the trailerites shared. Its key elements were freedom and economy.

Freedom was first and foremost: the freedom to choose your destination, your climate, your style of dress, your next-door neighbor, your job. The freedom to change that fixed trajectory you were born into, that path you were set upon by parents and neighbors and teachers, by the whole well-meaning but sometimes misguided milieu of your childhood. The freedom to move away from your past, to shatter an inherited life style and take the pieces elsewhere and assemble them anew.

Rich and poor alike responded to this urge. Not that the trailerites sought any kind of radical break from society, as so many observers, particularly before the war, seemed to fear. Theirs was to some degree an adolescent rebellion, a superficial rebellion, a rebellion of style rather than content. They might make a great show of selling out and hitching up and leaving town in disgust, but they took, in their light baggage, most of the town's basic values with them. The trailerite's median age was somewhere in the forties; they were, on the whole, too mature to confuse freedom with license. What most of these people sought from trailer living was simply a looser noose, the sort of freedom that Robert Frost defined as "pulling in easy harness."

Sociologists at first worried that the ready mobility of trailer life would lead to anonymity and irresponsibility and ultimate social breakdown; but they were largely disappointed in their predictions. For the wild-eyed and rebellious trailerites—even before the sobering events of Pearl Harbor—proved to be just as susceptible as anyone else to what the neighbors will think, if not more so. Life in the parks was actually far more public, more communal, more transparent than life in private houses and city apartments. The trailerites, in their little

"If there is a common road down which all these vehicles have traveled, it is a dual highway of security and independence."
—"At Home on the Highway," Roger B. White, *American Heritage,* December 1985

masonite fishbowls, lived a daily routine that was judged each evening over half a dozen dinner tables by a jury of their peers. Their freedom came from getting to choose their own jury.

The small town openness of the parks kept crime to a minimum. Right from the start, a few petty crooks and "rapscallions" (a nice thirties word) were able to adapt the trailer to their needs, but they seldom found the parks congenial: people there asked too many innocent questions, paid too much attention to everybody's comings and goings. Too, the parks were the juncture points of the trailerite grapevine, and trailer society was much smaller and tighter before the war than the news media, with its talk of wandering millions, led people to believe. The result was that crime rates in the parks were, on the whole, lower than in the surrounding areas—a fact that still holds for most mobile home communities today.

But the freedom of trailer life was only half its appeal. Equally important was economy. From its inception, "full-timing" was almost unbelievably economical—cheaper by half than apartment living. At a time when the typical city flat began at around twenty dollars a month, park rent might be as little as a dollar a week, including water and garbage pickup and use of all park facilities: bathrooms and laundry rooms, shuffleboard court and community hall and lending library and even the telephone in the office. A trailer couple, according to *The New York Times* in 1936, could live quite comfortably for under twelve dollars a week, including money for the movies.

For the poor—the fruit tramp beside the river, the sage-brusher in his three-hundred-dollar rig at the back of the park—the marvelous economy of trailer life offered a chance to own, if not the land under their feet, at least the roof over their heads; it offered a taste of independence. But in prewar America you didn't have to be poor to value economy. Even the well-to-do trailerites loved to boast about their low overhead; never before in the history of the middle class had romance and adventure carried such a modest price tag.

To the pioneers who founded the movement in the thirties, to wartime defense workers a thousand miles from home, to the people like Stanley and Dorena Ames, who signed on in the fifties, just as trailer life was dying and the press was rediscovering it, the trailer made sense.

"$25 REWARD for information leading to the recovery of 1937 Covered Wagon Deluxe Model, grey steel exterior, breakfast nook front end, SERIAL NO. D31129. Towed by blue 1937 Chevrolet coupe. Driven by Edward T. Schench, short, dark complexion, moustache. Sells hospital anaesthetic equipment—travels with wife. Last heard New York but may be in south headed north. Wire Chas. Witte, 3536 N. Nottingham Ave., Chicago."
—*Trailer Topics*, March 1939

"Most of these people have seen hard times. Drastically cutting the cost of living, trailer life enables them to pay off debts and get back on their feet."
—*Reader's Digest*, October 1941

It evolved from simpler needs in a simpler time, and while that time lasted, it satisfied the dreams of millions.

That time is gone, now, and thankfully. Few people would willingly return to so tenuous or so homely a life. Despite over a half-century of Social Security, few of us are that socially secure. All the more reason to remember—along with the pioneers, the sodbusters, the cowboys, and the Basque sheepherders—those hardy old trailerites, with their canaries and their barometers, their cotton rags and their little cans of Three-in-One Oil, out there polishing the hubcaps and oiling the hitch and jabbering with the neighbors from Pennsylvania thirty feet away and doing exactly the same thing.

"They are, perhaps, a new breed upon the earth."
—"Don't Call Them Trailer Trash," *The Saturday Evening Post*, August 2, 1952

Epilogue

Now it's over—two years of research, two years of scribbling about a piece of the past that's dead and gone. Two years of following up on leads from "friends and other strangers" (Bob Dylan) who want so much to be helpful, who grab your elbow and say "You've just *got* to talk to my wife's uncle down in Georgetown—he's lived in trailers all his life!" Leads that usually go nowhere (the wife's uncle bought his first "trailer"—a fourteen-by-sixty mobile home—twelve years ago, when he retired from the railroad). Two years of trying to redraw, from memory and old magazines, a picture of a gone world, a period of history both distinct and extinct, a time and a people as sharply circumscribed as, say, the era of the California gold rush, or the Pony Express, or the Texas cattle drives, or the building of the railroads. The trailerite subculture came and went within the twenty-five year span between 1935 and 1960. Like one of my childhood playmates, a petite and beautiful brown-eyed girl who died at eighteen of cystic fibrosis, the trailerites have been gone now much longer than they were here, and no amount of fingering their faded photographs, no amount of sifting and sorting and dissecting their curious histories, will ever bring them back.

I was concerned that they not be forgotten, or remembered merely as the butt of jokes—Lucille Ball and Desi Arnez doing their late movie pratfalls in *The Long, Long Trailer*—but as real people who woke up to a changing world and were alive and flexible enough to change with it. To change ahead of it, even.

I was concerned, too, to find an epitaph for these people, this race of indigenous American gypsies, and instead I found a thousand. The book is peppered with epitaphs, any one of which might serve to remember them by: A "shirt-sleeve society" they certainly were, as the *Christian Science Monitor* said; a people with a "wish to live unfettered," as Philip Smith pointed out in *Harper's*. They were also a "great wheeled

190

democracy" with "a passion for material comforts" (*The New York Times*). They simplified their lives only to complicate their dotted line, their horizontal roots, their personal histories. They gave up the middle-class prerogative of filling closets and attics and basements with useless impedimentia for the right to live like bums or gentlemen tramps—and buy a shiny new automobile every year or two with the money they saved.

The city of Detroit's charges against them, quoted in *Newsweek* in 1937, were largely true: their parks did look "like circus grounds;" and of course they "gossiped on their steps and helped one another with the laundry." They were *people* people rather than *thing* people, and their parks—matriarchal enclaves where women and children both dominated and predominated—showed it. They were a society built around mothers and kids and old folk, a society in which getting and spending, moving and shaking, took a back seat to "visiting," to simply living.

"Me and Ma got tired of settin' home wonderin' what to do until the undertaker come," an old carpenter from Indiana told a *Saturday Evening Post* reporter in Florida in 1936, speaking an epitaph for the million or more retirees who lived—and ultimately died—on wheels. Park life was good for the elderly—cozy and warm and carefree and communal. The luckiest ones were out greasing their hitches the day before the undertaker came.

James Jones, writing in *Holiday* in 1951 about the warmth and openness of a particular trailer court he remembered in Tucson, put it quite simply: "There was a curious sense of closeness and intimacy about the whole park, and anyone who came there immediately became a part of it. It was the antithesis of a New York apartment house." For the trailerites, or most of them, really were "friendly and gregarious . . . fraternizing on terms of equality" with everyone in camp. First, last, and always, they were tin can tourists, voluntary members of that great Elks lodge of the road—strangers to the townfolk, perhaps, but always at home among themselves wherever they went. Proud of their cars, proud of their trailers, but prouder still of their independence, their freedom, their ability to roll with almost any punch: whether for a strike, or a hurricane, or just a rumor of greener pastures, "We can be outa here by noon."

Almost a century before the first trailerite appeared, a young man from Massachusetts named Henry Thoreau withdrew—recoiled, actually—from the turbulent mainstream of American life and set about to blaze his own separate path to heaven. He distilled much of the wisdom of his journey into the book he called *Walden, or My Life in the Woods*. His principal advice is that we ought to follow our own genius and not knuckle under to the opinions of the world. With this the old trailerites, the pioneers, would certainly agree. "Simplify, simplify," Thoreau councils; "Let your affairs be as ones and twos, not as tens and hundreds," and again a million heads in the shade of a half-million striped awnings would nod their assent.

Those awnings are all gone now, and many of the heads that sat beneath them have passed into a deeper, cooler shade. But not before they were blessed to be able to follow, however briefly, Thoreau's most difficult admonition in *Walden*: "For as long as possible," he said, "live free."

And this, ultimately, may be all the epitaph the trailerites need.

Selected Bibliography

Baker, Ralph, "Home, Sweet Home Goes on the Road," *American Mercury*, September 1935, pp. 103ff.

Boone, Andrew R. "Modern Gypsies," *Popular Science Monthly* (April 1936), pp. 29ff.

Calkins, Earnest Elmo, "Rolling Homes and Rolling Stones," *The Rotarian* (July 1937), pp. 14ff.

Cooper, Morley, *The Trailer Book* (New York: Harper & Brothers, 1950).

Cowgill, Donald O., *Mobile Homes* (Philadelphia: University of Pennsylvania Press, 1941).

Edwards, Carlton, *Homes for Travel and Living* (East Lansing: privately published, 1977).

Evans, Ernestine, "Resettlement by Trailer," *The Nation* (August 15, 1936) pp. 180ff.

Harvey, W. Clifford, "Back to the Covered Wagon," *Christian Science Monitor Magazine* (October 7, 1936), pp. 3–4.

"Hitting the Trail—1935 Style," *Popular Mechanics* (July 1935), pp. 40ff.

Jessup, Elon, *The Motor-Camping Book* (New York: G. P. Putnam's Sons, 1921).

Jones, James, "Living in a Trailer," *Holiday* (August 1951), pp. 74ff.

MacDowell, Syl, *We Live in a Trailer* (New York: Julian Messner, 1938).

Marsh, Freeman, *Trailers* (New York: Coward-McCann, 1937).

Martin, Harold H., "Don't Call Them Trailer Trash," *The Saturday Evening Post* (August 2, 1952), pp. 24ff.

Meloan, Taylor W. *Mobile Homes* (Homewood, Illinois: Richard D. Irwin, Inc., 1954).

Nash, Charles Edward, *Trailer Ahoy!* (Lancaster: The Intelligencer Publishing Co., 1937).

Saunders, Lawrence, "Roll Your Own Home," *The Saturday Evening Post* (May 23, 1936), pp. 12ff.

Sims, Blackburn, *The Trailer Home* (New York: Longmans, Green & Co., 1937).

Smith, Philip H. "After Cars Come Trailers," *Scientific American* (February 1937), pp. 94–95.

————. "Where is the Trailer Going?" *SAE Transactions* (February 1937), pp. 45ff.

"Tin Canners," *Literary Digest* (August 15, 1936), p. 7.

"Two Hundred Thousand Trailers," *Fortune* (March 1937), pp. 105ff.

Wilson, Alice, "You Can Take 'Em with You," *The Saturday Evening Post* (August 14, 1937), pp. 7ff.

Index